COUNTRY STORE ANTIQUES

From Cradles to Caskets

Douglas Congdon-Martin
With Robert Biondi

Dedication
To Harold and Margaret Martin, my parents,
who have kept alive the tradition of shopkeeping.
In their stores and with their lives
they have embodied the ideal of service to others.
Thanks.

Published by Schiffer Publishing, Ltd.
1469 Morstein Road
West Chester, Pennsylvania 19380
Please write for a free catalog.
This book may be purchased from the publisher.
Please include $2.00 postage.
Try your bookstore first.

Printed in the United States of America.
ISBN: 0-88740-331-X

We are interested in hearing from authors with book
ideas on related topics.

Acknowledgments

There are a number of people to thank for their involvement with this book. Without their assistance, support, and willingness to share their collections and information, it would not have been possible.

Hearing a report on National Public Radio about a country store in Chapel Hill, North Carolina, I ventured a phone call to John and Elsie Booker. Two weeks later I met them face to face, and their openness and help has led not to one, but two books. They allowed us free reign of the Patterson's Mill Country Store for several days to capture it on film. They were there with information and a ready dust cloth, ladder, or screw driver. They have also been free with encouragement and prayers as the book slowly took shape. I thank them.

The Bookers were also responsible for introducing us to Frank and Betty Lou Gay who opened their home and wonderful collection to us. They took a day from their own work to work with us, helping us to rearrange their dining room to create a studio, and sharing a wealth of information and hospitality with us as we photographed.

I met Cindy Marsh and Ron Koehler at the advertising show in Indianapolis. They knew I was working on a book and suggested that I come to visit their shop in Lafayette, Indiana. About a year later I dug their card out of my desk drawer and gave them a call. They renewed the invitation and we spent two very full days in their wonderful shop. Koehler Bros. Inc.—The General Store is filled from floor to ceiling with a great variety of country store antiques, and everything is for sale. It is the kind of place a collector should make every effort to visit.

Back in North Carolina, Faye and John Cooper, the current owners of Mast General Store in Valle Crucis, welcomed us into their world. This is an authentic country store. It welcomes tourists, attracting them from around the country to crowd its aisles. But early in the morning, when we arrived to start our work, the residents of Valle Crucis were gathered there. They came to pick up their mail, buy the morning paper, and sit around the potbellied stove to catch up on the news. While the tourists were just beginning to stir from their sleep, the local customers picked up their groceries and went about their day's work. It was a real dose of the country store spirit, and I thank John and Faye for it.

Not too far from Valle Crucis is Todd, North Carolina. We heard about another active general store there, and stopped in on our way home. John and Sheila Morgan had no idea who we were, but allowed us to explore their collections and take pictures. We hope that if there is another book we can spend some more time there.

Along the way others have opened their collections and shops to us. We appreciate their generosity. They include: Nancy Buchanan, Olde Treasure Shoppe Antiques, Andover, Massachusetts; Gary Metz, Muddy River Trading Company, Roanoke, Virginia; and the Hook's Historic Drug Store & Pharmacy Museum, Indianapolis, Indiana.

One of the main contributors to the first country store book we did, *Country Store Collectibles*, was Mary Lou Holt. While her collection does not appear here, she played a key role in this book by introducing me to Tom Clark's book *Pills, Petticoats, and Plows*, which has been a source of information and inspiration for this work (it is available from the University of Oklahoma Press, Norman, Oklahoma). Mary Lou has been a constant source of encouragement and support, and I thank her.

Bob Biondi and Kate Dooner of the Schiffer team were of great assistance in gathering information and photography. Ellen J. (Sue) Taylor brought her skill and artistry to the design of the book.

As always, a book like this arises out of the shared interest and energy of many people. I thank them all.

Douglas Congdon-Martin
West Chester, Pennsylvania

Contents

Introduction 7
From Cradles to Caskets

Chapter One: **"If You Can't Buy it Here, You Don't Need It"** 9

Chapter Two: **The Stuff of Life** 26
Baking Powder 26
Beans 31
Biscuits and Crackers 32
Bread 36
Cereals 38
Cocoa 41
Coffee and Tea 43
Dairy Products and Eggs 62
Lard and Shortening 64
Spices 66
Other Foods 70

Chapter Three: **Sweets and Treats** 74
Ice Cream and Candy 74
Peanuts and Peanut Butter 79
Soft Drinks 83

Chapter Four: **Smokes and Spirits** 88
Tobacco 88
Spirits 106

Chapter Five: **Head to Toe, Inside and Out** . . . .
Clothing 109
Shoes 113
Remedies 118
Toys 120

Chapter Six: **Everything for the Home, Road, and Farm** 123
Around the Kitchen 123
Laundry Day 131
Household Goods 135
Dyes and Notions 140
Hardware 144
Lighting 147
Automobiles 150
Farm Needs 151

Bibliography 160

Opposite page top:
Country store interior from the turn of the century.

Opposite page bottom:
From the well-stocked shelves to the candy jars on the counter, this photo of a store from 1905 gives a feel for the country store as it really was.

You can see the pride on the face of this shopkeeper of a general store. Even though this is obviously a general store in a more urban setting, the proprietor of the store was at the center of his community's life, and played an important role in its economic health. Notice the men in the suits sitting by the potbellied stove. You can take the man out of the country, but you can't take the country out of the man.

Introduction
FROM CRADLES TO CASKETS

In the world of collecting there is probably no category as broad as country store antiques. It was the nature and mission of the country store to meet every need a person might have during his or her life. One country store, still in operation, has carried literally everything "from cradles to caskets" in the course of its history.

So it is not surprising that the field of country store antiques, include tins and bins, tobacco, advertising, packaging, store equipment, washboards, irons, lighting, sewing machines, automobilia, farm equipment and supplies, breweriana, clothing, and other items that can be seen on the pages that follow. There are, of course, collectors who focus their efforts in one or more of these areas, and they will find much to interest them in this book.

But true country store collectors are eclectics. They are not happy with specialization. They need variety to keep them going. They are constantly on the lookout for the best, the rarest, the most beautiful, and sometimes the weirdest. The taste of country store collectors is as varied as the stores themselves. I suspect that when they are not collecting they can be found in the local hardware store wandering about the aisles, not looking for anything in particular, but feeling a sense of awe at the clever minds that created all those wonderful, varied things. They are addicted, and lacking an antique shop or show, the hardware store gives them a quick fix.

I am a country store junkie, and it is a habit I am not in a hurry to break. As many objects as I have seen and touched in the course of writing two books on the subject, and as many stores as I have visited, I still feel the excitement when I enter a store. I know that I will be surprised by something I have never seen before or amazed by the ingenuity of some creative soul who lived a hundred years ago. For an unabashed eclectic, the country store offers a thrill a minute!

If you have bought this book and read this far, I assume we share a common affliction, interest, and love. I hope the pages that follow bring you as much pleasure and knowledge as putting them together has brought to me. Here you will find the remnants of a simpler time, objects that filled the shelves, counters, walls, and floors of the country stores. Today they are cherished mementos, highly valued antiques, that trace not only the history of the stores, but our own as well. Enjoy!

"An Old Fashioned New England Grocery." This print was given with the compliments of Chase and Sanborn Coffee, 1897. Lithograph by Abbott Graves. Paper, 23.5" x 19.5". *Courtesy of the Olde Treasure Shoppe, Andover, Massachusetts.*

The entrance to Koehler's Country Store has this sleigh from the H.E. McDonald Company, probably used for winter deliveries.

Chapter One
"If You Can't Buy it Here, You Don't Need It"

While the country store can trace its genealogy to the earliest trading posts on the continent, it came into its own after the Civil War. In the last half of the nineteenth century, there was a growth spurt of stores. At every promising crossroad, every new railroad stop, some enterprising entrepreneur set up his stand.

In his classic work, *Pills, Petticoats, & Plows: The Southern Country Store*, Thomas D. Clark identified several factors in this growth. While his work focuses principally on the Southern experience, it is safe to assume that, with some variations, the same forces were at work in the North and the West. With the war over, veterans were looking for ways to make their livings. While many returned to the farms or the trades they had left behind, others sought new ventures.

Yankee soldiers saw the South as "a land of opportunity," according to Clark, and they returned after the war to set up their businesses. [1] Many had made friendships with the people when they were occupying soldiers, and were welcomed back as members of the community.

Confederate veterans turned to shopkeeping after returning home to find their plantations in disarray. [2] Others, North and South, had left stores in the hands of wives or mothers, and returned with renewed energy, to revive the business.

Stores were also started by the peddlers who carted their wares about the countryside in wagons. The roads ranged from bad to worse and the peddlers were always looking for a place to settle down. They had the advantage of experience. According to Clark, they already knew the trade. "Old friends who had traded generously with them in their horse-and-wagon days, were given slight advantages of lower prices and, frequently, little presents of lagniappes for old times sake." [3]

That many of these entrepreneurs met success is a testament to the pent-up consumer demand after the sacrifices of the war years. They were anxious to buy, and willing to go into debt to do it. It was an environment where, with just a minimum of business sense and an understanding of what the customer wanted, the owner of a country store could build a thriving business.

The growth of country stores in the late 1800s was an important element in the economic development of the nation. They were the keystone that supported the commerce system. On their porches and in their aisles local products were exchanged for manufactured goods, and both the farmers and the manufacturers depended on the stores to reach a larger and profitable market.

To the farmers, the stores offered a system of credit that allowed them to survive until the crop was harvested. The storekeeper knew the farmers and their farms well. He used this knowledge to estimate the harvest of a particular farm and set a monthly credit limit based on that projection. The farmer could borrow against the credit limit in the form of goods or money through the winter months and growing season. At harvest time the farmer would bring the produce to the store, where the storekeeper would credit their accounts. The storekeeper would then sell the cotton, grain, or other produce, usually at a substantial profit.

When the harvest was good the country store prospered. Money was made by adding a premium to the price for privilege of credit, by charging interest on borrowed money, and by reselling crops at a substantial mark-up. Some contemporary newspapers occasionally accused a storekeeper of usury, but few people ever complained. So essential was the store's role in the well-being of the community, that, as long as the proprietor was fair and even-handed, the people were grateful to him. They understood that the store was taking on a lot of risk. As Clark explains:

"A general crop failure promised ruin for the store and certainly bankruptcy for the customer. The sudden disappearance or death of a customer was a blow to a storekeeper's business...A hundred credit customers who religiously settled their accounts at the end of each crop season were often forced to pay the accounts of another hundred who did not...Both merchant and customer were clear on the point that good risks had to be responsible for the bad ones." [4]

On the other side of the country store keystone were the manufacturers of the myriad of goods that filled the shelves and aisles. In the years after the Civil War, the industrial revolution took hold in America. The economy began to change, moving toward a greater interdependence of various segments of society. The isolation of country folks, who grew or made nearly everything they needed for survival, began to be broken. The manufactured goods they found at the country stores offered them the luxury of time and relief from some of their labors. At the same

The Mast General Store in Valle Crucis, North Carolina has been in operation at this location since 1882. Now on the National Register of Historic Places, it continues to serve the community, while having a great appeal to tourists visiting the area. *Courtesy of the Mast General Store, Valle Crucis, North Carolina.*

time, the country store, by buying their crops, was the source of the cash that allowed them to participate in the new economy.

The manufacturers did not miss this fact. The stores were the "heartbeat and pulse of a good portion of American business,"[5] selling millions of dollars of goods each year. In the major cities trade centers were established, where country storekeepers could find the latest merchandise for their stores. The trips to these mercantile Meccas were an adventure for the storekeeper and his family. Their transportation and lodging often paid for, they were treated as the important link in the chain of commerce they were.

The other way manufacturers and wholesalers got their goods out was through an army of drummers going from store to store. These salesmen were welcomed visitors. Along with the latest goods, gizmos, and gadgets, they brought stories of the larger world and yarns that would keep the gathering around the stove entertained for hours on end. At the same time they would gather information for their employers. They kept track of the economy, the anticipated crops, and the credit-worthiness of the stores. While part of their job was to post the signs and advertisements that helped create the market for their products, their main concern was building up a trusting and profitable relationship with the merchant. As Clark describes it, drummers "became almost as much a part of the store business as were the cat and stove."[6]

The country store was typically one of the central buildings in the community. Along with the church and the courthouse, it stood at the spiritual center of the town. Country store architecture was plain and functional. Most often it was a two-storied structure, with the second floor rented by a lodge or church for its meetings. Many stores wore square false fronts, to give them the dignified appearance worthy of their place in the community.

Nearly every country store had a large porch across its front. Its architectural function was to facilitate the loading and unloading of wagons. But, more importantly, it was the gathering place where the farmers, who came into town on Saturday to trade, could greet their neighbors and catch up on the news. Many community issues were debated and settled there by people sitting on rocking chairs, benches, or barrels. Politicians would use the country store porch as a rostrum for their speeches. The porches were also an ideal place for observing the weather, philosophizing about religion, or acting out the rituals of courtship.

When the weather turned, the functions of the porch were transferred to the stove. Located at the center of the store, it was surrounded by open, communal space. Chairs or benches surrounded it, and they were usually filled by people whittling, playing checkers, talking, or simply rocking while enjoying a good chew. The stove was a great target for tobacco chewers, and gave off a gratifying hiss when it was hit.

Though the shopkeeper sometimes had to evict the laggard who sat all day nibbling from the cracker barrel while buying nothing, the attraction of the stove was a boon to business. It brought people into the store and kept them there long enough for them to remember what they needed to buy. Occasionally, however, the social life around the stove was too much for the shopkeeper. Clark reports that "a storekeeper, in idle moments, often fell victim to checkerboards and card playing and allowed these frivolities to interfere seriously with the conduct of his business. It was not unusual for a merchant to deny that he had

The front porch of the country store was the place where much of the commerce and social life of the community took place. *Courtesy of John & Elsie Booker, Patterson's Mill Country Store, Chapel Hill.*

The Hackney Wagon Company of Wilson, North Carolina capitalized on the popularity of the country store porch by providing seating with advertising. *Courtesy of John & Elsie Booker, Patterson's Mill Country Store, Chapel Hill.*

The pot bellied stove is at the center of the store, and local people still gather around it to exchange news and pleasantries. *Courtesy of the Mast General Store, Valle Crucis, North Carolina.*

Around the stove are arranged comfortable chairs and a checker board that, in the traditional way, uses bottle caps as playing pieces. *Courtesy of the Mast General Store, Valle Crucis, North Carolina.*

The exterior Todd's General Store. Like the Mast store, Todd's General Store is a living heritage, serving the community while peeking the interest of tourists. *Courtesy of the Todd General Store, Todd, North Carolina.*

Todd's store also has the stove in the center surrounded by benches. *Courtesy of the Todd General Store, Todd, North Carolina.*

certain articles in stock when a pestiferous customer insisted that he leave a game to wait upon him."[7]

The other great trade stimulator in country stores was the post office. It usually stood near the front entrance or on the back wall. With its barred window and locked boxes, it looked very official, which it was. Even in the most remote outpost of civilization the presence of the federal government was present in the form of the post office. It was a comforting thought.

As the postmaster, the storekeeper had another vital role in the community, but not one without conflict. With the advent of the great catalog houses like Sears, Roebuck & Co. and Montgomery Ward, the storekeeper was in the position of helping the competition. Not only did he have to post the orders, but often he was called upon to issue a money order on his customer's credit.

Shelving stretched across the walls of the country store from floor to ceiling. Organized by the type of merchandise they carried, one section would carry grocery items, another hardware, and another clothing. In a ring in front of the shelves stood the counters over which sales were transacted. These counters were often made by local craftsmen. They had broad surfaces which were cluttered with, among other things, advertising, cash registers, paper racks and string dispensers, ribbon cases, candy jars, and tobacco counter tins. Underneath the counters were ample shelves and, if the carpenter were clever enough, bins for dispensing flour, sugar, and grains. Really fancy shelves had slanting fronts with bins for various foods, with the food neatly displayed in the window of the bin.

If the store were large enough, it may have had islands of counters in the center of the store. These often had glass sides so the customer could see the array of goods displayed inside. Scattered among the aisles were crates and barrels filled with crackers, pickles, whiskey, kerosene, molasses, and other products which were dispensed into containers to be carried home.

Typical of many country stores was the W.W. Mast General Store in Valle Crucis, North Carolina. Still a thriving enterprise, it is listed in the National Register of Historic Places as one of the finest remaining examples of an old country general store.[8]

The first building of the present store was built in 1882 by Henry Taylor, who had operated a smaller store across the street for many years. W.W. Mast bought half interest in the store in 1897, and the store became known as Taylor & Mast General Merchandise. Mast soon bought Taylor's interest in the store, and it was owned and managed by the Mast family for sixty years.

When discussing his philosophy of merchandizing, W.W. Mast was well known for saying "If you can't buy it here, you don't need it." He stocked everything the community might need from "cradles to caskets," and, indeed, there is still a casket in the second floor salesroom. As in other country stores credit was the normal way of business, and Mast accepted produce, roots and herbs, and chickens in payment for his goods. There was a trap door in the floor of the store so a chicken could be weighed and dropped into the coop. It is still there in case, the current owners say, "we decide to return to the barter system."

In Chapel Hill, North Carolina, John and Elsie Booker have recreated a country store near the site of one of the earliest in the area. Patterson's Mill Country Store captures the chaotic charm of the old store, from its broad, welcoming front porch, to the shelves stocked with antique containers and packaging. The

The original post office in the front corner of the Mast General Store still functions, serving the needs of the community. *Courtesy of the Mast General Store, Valle Crucis, North Carolina.*

13

This view from the balcony of Patterson's Mill Country Store gives some sense of the atmosphere of these places, the intriguing clutter of merchandise amidst the warm woods and bright advertising.

Another view of the main sales area of Patterson's Mill Country Store.

Booker's years of collecting country store items are on display in every corner, on every wall, and even from the ceilings, making it a point of reference for other collectors. Thousands of visitors each year take a step back into history, remembering their childhoods or the stories from parents and grandparents. They are able to buy a cold soda, a bag of peanuts, candies, one of the many locally crafted gifts, or one of the antiques that are for sale.

In 1914 Todd, North Carolina was a hub of activity. The Norfolk and Western Railroad had opened its line from Abington, Virginia to Todd, and the future was promising. It became a center for the timber industry in North Carolina, and suddenly sprouted two hotels, nine stores, a bank, four doctors, a dentist, a Masonic Lodge, Odd Fellow's Hall, a post office, a drugstore, a mill, and even a "rent-a-buggy" service. This prosperity continued well into the 1930s, when the timber was

Todd store carries country store antiques as well as the day-to-day groceries and other goods the community needs and quality items for tourists. *Courtesy of the Todd General Store, Todd, North Carolina.*

played out and the economy entered into depression. Finally, in 1940, a devastating flood brought the end of Todd's boom period.[9]

Todd, however, has survived, and its people continue to be vital, vibrant folk, who still trade at one of the stores founded in 1914. Todd General Store has served continuously in the same location, with the exception of four brief months in 1985 before its present owners, Joe and Sheila Morgan, took over its management. When they arrived it had been stripped of most of its contents, but the broad porch remained as did much of the spirit of the place. Through their love of country store antiques and a lot of dedication, they have built a business that serves the local community and the tourist trade alike.

A bit farther north, in Lafayette, Indiana, one finds the General Store at Koehler Bros. Inc. While it is not operating as a country store, Cindy Marsh and Ron Koehler have gathered together a wonderful collection of country store antiques for sale to the public. Here are the counters, advertising, containers, and equipment that give the stores their character, all housed in a building that captures the country store milieu.

These are but a few of hundreds of country stores that can be found around the country. Many have uninterrupted histories, and the ghosts of former customers and merchants can almost be heard walking about the aisles. Others pay homage to a by-gone era, faithfully reproducing the physical and spiritual reality that was the country store. Old and new alike, they awaken in us a spark of remembrance of a simpler time, a time when the places of business were more human and community was more manifest.

Wood and glass display counter. Burge-Huck Manufacturing Co., Quincy, Illinois. 44″ x 55″ x 26″. *Courtesy of Koehler Bros. Inc.—The General Store, Lafayette, Indiana.*

FOOTNOTES

[1] Thomas D. Clark, *Pills, Petticoats, and Plows: The Southern Country Store*, (Norman, Oklahoma: University of Oklahoma Press, 1944.), p. 6.

[2] *Ibid.*, p. 7.

[3] *Ibid.*, p. 8.

[4] *Ibid.*, p. 274.

[5] *Ibid.*, p. 15.

[6] *Ibid.*, p. 93.

[7] *Ibid.*, p. 36.

[8] From a brochure published by the Mast General Store, p. 2.

[9] From an undated, unattributed article about Todd's history by Linda F. Nicholson.

Long wood counter, with the original red paint on the base. 33″ x 115″ x 36″. *Courtesy of Koehler Bros. Inc.—The General Store, Lafayette, Indiana.*

Walnut display cabinet by Rothschild's Sons Co., Cincinnati. 49″ x 23″ x 16″. *Courtesy of Koehler Bros. Inc.—The General Store, Lafayette, Indiana.*

Glass and wood ribbon case with three sections that open up as seen here. Exhibition Showcase Co., Erie, Pennsylvania. 50″ x 26″ x 23″. *Courtesy of Koehler Bros. Inc.—The General Store, Lafayette, Indiana.*

This maple counter has nice shelf space below with glass doors. 32″ x 45″ x 30″. *Courtesy of Koehler Bros. Inc.—The General Store, Lafayette, Indiana.*

A slant-front seed counter in oak with eighteen glass doors. Each has decal of the seed within. 32″ x 45″ x 30″. *Courtesy of Koehler Bros. Inc.—The General Store, Lafayette, Indiana.*

A beautiful glass and wood display case with tiered wooden shelves for the display of items. 36" x 7'10" x 23". Courtesy of Koehler Bros. Inc.—The General Store, Lafayette, Indiana.

Seed counter, 34" x 116" x 25". Courtesy of Koehler Bros. Inc.—The General Store, Lafayette, Indiana.

Counter string dispenser. Iron and wire, 21″ x 12″. *Courtesy of Koehler Bros. Inc.—The General Store, Lafayette, Indiana.*

Oak and brass Peek's Cash Register, no. 2651, Manufactured by A.R. Peek, Cortland, New York. Its patent dates are 1888 and 1889. *Courtesy of Betty Lou and Frank Gay.*

Balance scale by Henry Troemner, Philadelphia. Iron and brass, 10″ x 27″ x 13″. *Courtesy of Koehler Bros. Inc.—The General Store, Lafayette, Indiana.*

This flour sifter/dispenser bears the advertising of the Parker Brothers Cash Store in Cato, New York where it once hung. *Courtesy of Betty Lou and Frank Gay.*

Miniature salesman's sample of a meat counter. Wood, glass, and metal, 9.5″ x 30″ x 9″. *Courtesy of Koehler Bros. Inc.--The General Store, Lafayette, Indiana.*

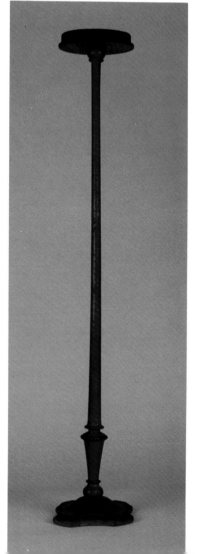

Walnut hat stand, 30.5″ x 5″. *Courtesy of Koehler Bros. Inc.— The General Store, Lafayette, Indiana.*

Jewelry case of wood and glass with a nice tree of shelves. In the austerity of country life, jewelry was a welcome luxury, and one of the key products carried in country stores. 33.5″ x 18″ x 18″. *Courtesy of Koehler Bros. Inc.—The General Store, Lafayette, Indiana.*

A more modern store cooler was this General Electric refrigerator. Steel cabinet on cast iron legs, 64″ x 28″ x 22.5″. *Courtesy of John & Elsie Booker, Patterson's Mill Country Store, Chapel Hill.*

This oak and glass ice box held a huge block of ice. The curved glass and beautiful cabinet work speaks of the ingenuity and care involved in its creation. 81″ x 45″ x 44″. *Courtesy of John & Elsie Booker, Patterson's Mill Country Store, Chapel Hill.*

A combination cash box and display counter. Wood and glass, 11.5″ x 51.5″ x 22″. *Courtesy of John & Elsie Booker, Patterson's Mill Country Store, Chapel Hill.*

Wood grained tin cash register on an oak base. The register was operated by a lever which one would slide to the appropriate number before pulling a handle to record the sale. 17″ x 9″ x 17″. *Courtesy of the Mast General Store, Valle Crucis, North Carolina.*

A National cash register that once stood in the store of G.H. Ray. Cast brass, 21″ x 17.5″ x 16″. *Courtesy of John & Elsie Booker, Patterson's Mill Country Store, Chapel Hill.*

A three roll paper stand in cast iron with an enameled sign for Major's Cement 10 & 15. *Courtesy of Betty Lou and Frank Gay.*

Assorted string holders, 6″ x 11″. *Courtesy of the Mast General Store, Valle Crucis, North Carolina.*

REX paper stand and cutter, 13″ x 24.5″. *Courtesy of the Mast General Store, Valle Crucis, North Carolina.*

Cast iron and wood paper stand and cutter, 12″ x 15.5″. *Courtesy of the Mast General Store, Valle Crucis, North Carolina.*

Cast iron umbrella and cane stand. B.C. Tatum Co., c. 1885. 28″. *Courtesy of the Mast General Store, Valle Crucis, North Carolina.*

Revolving oak ribbon dispenser. 39″ tall. *Courtesy of the Mast General Store, Valle Crucis, North Carolina.*

Bulk molasses came in barrels. To remove the molasses the store owner tapped the barrels with a pump like this one from the National Specialty Co., Philadelphia, c. 1908. The 18" barrel was from Covington's, Wilmington, North Carolina. *Courtesy of John & Elsie Booker, Patterson's Mill Country Store, Chapel Hill.*

This cheese slicer operated on the same principle as the Gem Computer. Cast iron and wood, 10" x 19" diameter. *Courtesy of the Mast General Store, Valle Crucis, North Carolina.*

Coin operated moving picture machine. For a penny, one could see one of five shows: "Charlie the Newsboy," "When Hidwilli Had a Fire," "Trimming a Fresh Bill," "Ole Olson the Bone-Headed Janitor," or "Roly Poly." All pictures were approved by New York and Chicago censors. Exhibit Supply Company, Chicago. 24" x 8.5" x 11". *Courtesy of John & Elsie Booker, Patterson's Mill Country Store, Chapel Hill.*

National grocery scale built by the Food Machines Division, Cincinnati Time Recorder Co., Cincinnati. 23.5″ x 19″. *Courtesy of the Mast General Store, Valle Crucis, North Carolina.*

The Gem Cheese Computer had a graduated wheel for the accurate measurement of cheese. The screened cabinet kept the flies away. The Standard Computing Scale Co., Ltd., Detroit, Michigan. Wood, glass, and screen, 14″ x 21.5″ x 26.5″. *Courtesy of the Mast General Store, Valle Crucis, North Carolina.*

Chapter Two

The Stuff of Life

BAKING POWDER

Assorted baking powder containers: Rumford Baking Powder wooden box, 4.5" x 8.5"; Rumford tin with paper label, 5.25"; Grand Union Tea Co., Brooklyn, New York, tin, 5.25"; New South Baking Powder tin, Knoxville, Tennessee. *Courtesy of John & Elsie Booker, Patterson's Mill Country Store, Chapel Hill.*

Various Calumet Baking Powder tins, 3.25-5.5" tall. The tins on the left and in the middle are the oldest, with the tin on the right coming next. Calumet Baking Powder Co., Chicago, Illinois. *Courtesy of John & Elsie Booker, Patterson's Mill Country Store, Chapel Hill.*

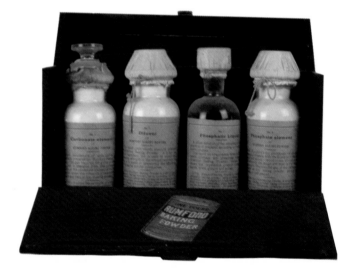

Though we take it for granted today, baking powder is actually a product of "modern" chemistry, discovered around 1850. The early drummers met resistance and skepticism to this newfangled food product, so they took a kit such as this one with them on sales calls. It has the basic ingredients of baking powder: Carbonate of Soda, which produces the carbon bubbles; corn starch (diluent), which absorbs water from the air to prevent an unwanted reaction; a phosphate which promotes the chemical reaction and an acid. When water is added to this it creates carbon gas bubbles which make the baked goods nice and light. Rumford Baking Powder, Rumford, Rhode Island, c. 1870. 8" x 11". *Courtesy of John & Elsie Booker, Patterson's Mill Country Store, Chapel Hill.*

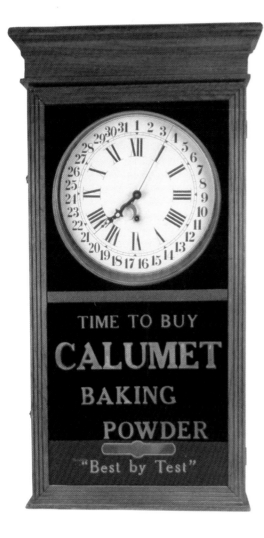

Clabber Girl Baking Powder tins. Hulman & Co., Terre Haute, Indiana, 4"-5.5". *Courtesy of John & Elsie Booker, Patterson's Mill Country Store, Chapel Hill.*

A nice Calumet pendulum clock in walnut and reverse painted glass. 34" x 18" x 5". *Courtesy of John & Elsie Booker, Patterson's Mill Country Store, Chapel Hill.*

Tins for Davis Baking Powder, R.G. Davis Company, Hoboken, New Jersey. L: lithographed tin, 7.25"; R: paper labeled tin, 5". *Courtesy of John & Elsie Booker, Patterson's Mill Country Store, Chapel Hill.*

27

Hearth Club Baking Powder tins. The older tin on the left is marked "Manufactured by Rumford Chemical Works, Rumford, Rhode Island" and measures 4.5". The other tin is marked "Distributed by Rumford Company...Terre Haute, Indiana" and is 9" tall. *Courtesy of John & Elsie Booker, Patterson's Mill Country Store, Chapel Hill.*

Left: This Peerless Baking Powder tin with paper label, 5.25", has an offer for a free spoon. Canby, Ach & Canby, Dayton, Ohio. Right: Royal Baking Powder tin, 4", New York, New York. *Courtesy of Koehler Bros. Inc.—The General Store, Lafayette, Indiana.*

K.C. Baking Powder tin, Jacques Mfg. Co., Chicago, 6.5". *Courtesy of John & Elsie Booker, Patterson's Mill Country Store, Chapel Hill.*

These Rough Rider Baking Powder tins have an image of a man who looks suspiciously like Teddy Roosevelt. This cleverly takes advantage of his hero status without actually having an endorsement of the product. The Southern Manufacturing Co., Richmond, Virginia, c. 1900, 4"-4.5". *Courtesy of John & Elsie Booker, Patterson's Mill Country Store, Chapel Hill.*

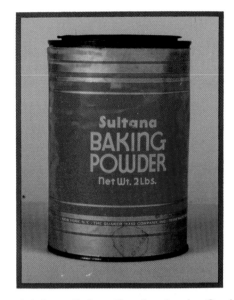

Snow King Baking Powder tins, 4.5"-5.5". The Snow King Baking Powder Co., Memphis, Tennessee. *Courtesy of John & Elsie Booker, Patterson's Mill Country Store, Chapel Hill.*

Two pound Sultana Baking Powder tin, the Quaker Maid Company, Inc., Terre Haute, Indiana. *Courtesy of John & Elsie Booker, Patterson's Mill Country Store, Chapel Hill.*

Tin and wire Snow King Baking Powder paper bag holder. 16.5" x 10". *Courtesy of Betty Lou and Frank Gay.*

Assorted baking powder tins. Top row (l-r): Donnell's, 5.5", paper label; Great Eastern, St. Louis, Missouri, paper label; Baker's, Springfield, Massachusetts, 5.25", paper label; Clabber Girl, copyright 1899, Hulman & Co., Terre Haute. Bottom row (l-r): KC, 6.75", paper label; Cleveland's, 5.25", paper label; Little Fairies, manufactured for Lincoln Chemical Works, Chicago, paper label; Snow King, 4.75", paper label. *Courtesy of Betty Lou and Frank Gay.*

Assorted baking powder tins. Top row (l-r): Sodarine, Baltimore, Maryland, 3.75", paper label; Royal, 1938, Standard Brands, 4"; Calumet, 4.25"; Good Luck in paper wrapper, 3.75". Bottom row (l-r): Parrot Monkey, 3.75", paper label; Rough Rider, Richmond, 4.25", paper label; Booster, 4"; Good Luck, Richmond, paper label, 4"; Davis, Penick & Ford Ltd., Hoboken, New Jersey, 4", paper label. *Courtesy of Betty Lou and Frank Gay.*

BEANS

Brown Heinz Oven Baked Beans crock, 10" x 12". Courtesy of Koehler Bros. Inc.—The General Store, Lafayette, Indiana.

Pottery Boston Baked Bean pot with raised letters and image on back. *Courtesy of Koehler Bros. Inc.—The General Store, Lafayette, Indiana.*

Nice three dimensional standing Van Camp's sign in cardboard. Gloechner & Faust, New York, 18″ x 28″. *Courtesy of Koehler Bros. Inc.—The General Store, Lafayette, Indiana.*

BISCUITS AND CRACKERS

Glass and wood counter jar with raised letters on four sides: Geo. A Bayle, St. Louis/Saratoga Chip Potatoes/Pretzels & Crackers/Salted Corn & Peanuts. 8″ x 6″ x 6″. *Courtesy of Gary Metz, Roanoke, Virginia.*

Wooden cracker crate for C.D. Boss & Son, New London, Connecticut. 10″ x 22″ x 14″. *Courtesy of Koehler Bros. Inc.—The General Store, Lafayette, Indiana.*

Donaldson Baking Company's Butter Cracker's tin, with a lithographed photo of their home delivery wagon. The Meekin Can Co., Cincinnati, Ohio, 7". *Courtesy of Betty Lou and Frank Gay.*

Oak and glass case for Fox Superior Crackers, Fort Wayne, Indiana, 32" x 23" x 23". *Courtesy of Koehler Bros. Inc.--The General Store, Lafayette, Indiana.*

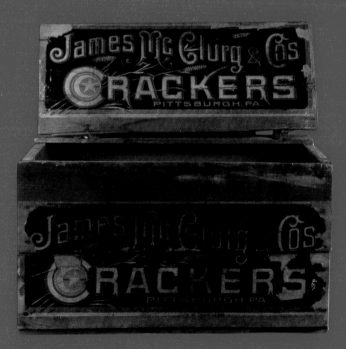

Cracker tins. Left: Edgemont Crackers by Green and Green Co., Dayton, Ohio, 7.75" x 7.25". Right: 9' Spanish-language Saltine's tin, Nabisco. *Courtesy of John & Elsie Booker, Patterson's Mill Country Store, Chapel Hill.*

Crate for James McClure & Co's Crackers, Pittsburgh, Pennsylvania. Wood with paper labels, 13.5" x 23.5" x 13.5". *Courtesy of Koehler Bros. Inc.—The General Store, Lafayette, Indiana.*

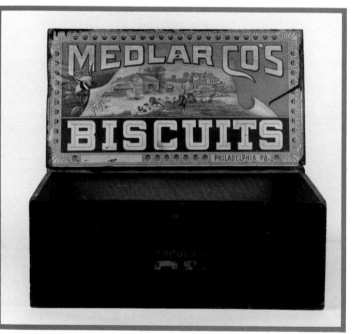

Paper poster for McVitie & Price Biscuits. 31″ x 24″.
*Courtesy of Koehler Bros. Inc.—The General Store,
Lafayette, Indiana.*

Medlar Co's Biscuits, Philadelphia, wooden crate with
lithographed paper label. Hinda, Ketcham & Co., Labela,
New York, 8″ x 22″ x 14″. *Courtesy of Koehler Bros. Inc.—
The General Store, Lafayette, Indiana.*

Large Uneeda Biscuit stand-up display. The National
Biscuit Company, 46″ x 15″. *Courtesy of Koehler Bros.
Inc.—The General Store, Lafayette, Indiana.*

34

Vitreous China Uneeda bowl made by J & E Mayer. 3" x 5".
*Courtesy of Koehler Bros. Inc.—The General Store,
Lafayette, Indiana.*

Ritz Cracker tin with Spanish language labels. Tin, 6" x 6".
*Courtesy of John & Elsie Booker, Patterson's Mill Country
Store, Chapel Hill.*

Cracker crate from W.S. Sands & Sons, Erie, Pennsylvania.
Wood with paper labels, 13" x 20" x 10". *Courtesy of
Koehler Bros. Inc.—The General Store, Lafayette, Indiana.*

Tin display rack for the Paul Schulze Biscuit Co., 42" x 17" x
16". *Courtesy of Koehler Bros. Inc.—The General Store,
Lafayette, Indiana.*

35

Wooden Stolzenbach Bakery Cracker & Cake crate with paper labels. 13" x 24" x 12.5". *Courtesy of Koehler Bros. Inc.--The General Store, Lafayette, Indiana.*

Lithographed National Biscuit Company tin for Welsh Rabbit Biscuits. 2" x 10" x 4.5". *Courtesy of Koehler Bros. Inc.--The General Store, Lafayette, Indiana.*

Tin and wood broom rack for Huber's Aunt Martha bread. 31" x 20". *Courtesy of Koehler Bros. Inc.—The General Store, Lafayette, Indiana.*

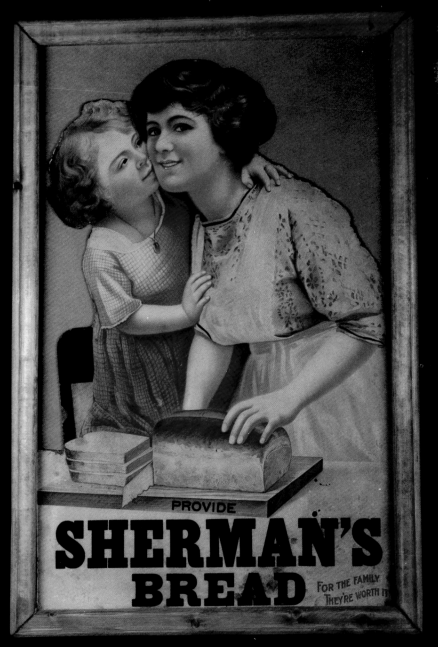

Die cut cardboard sign for Sherman's Bread, 1914. Kaufmann & Strauss Co., New York, 29″ x 20″. *Courtesy of Koehler Bros. Inc.—The General Store, Lafayette, Indiana.*

Broom rack advertising Bond Bread. Wood with an enameled steel sign, 41″ x 19″. *Courtesy of Koehler Bros. Inc.—The General Store, Lafayette, Indiana.*

CEREALS

Beautiful die cut Kellogg Corn Flakes sign. Cardboard, 34"
x 25". *Courtesy of Koehler Bros. Inc.—The General Store,
Lafayette, Indiana.*

Two-sided projecting wall sign, 1910. American Art Works, Coshocton, Ohio. Tin, 19" x 13.5". *Courtesy of Koehler Bros. Inc.—The General Store, Lafayette, Indiana.*

A nice collection of Quaker Oats containers at the Todd Country Store. *Courtesy of the Todd General Store, Todd, North Carolina.*

Tin for Quaker Rolled White Oats with Chinese language text on the back. 7.5" x 5". *Courtesy of Koehler Bros. Inc.—The General Store, Lafayette, Indiana.*

Post Toasties string holder. *Courtesy of Betty Lou and Frank Gay.*

COCOA

Assorted cocoa tins (l-r): Klein's Cocoa, Klein Chocolate Co., Elizabethtown, Pennsylvania, 7"; Dairy Maid, Newark, New Jersey, 5.5", paper label; Watkins Cocoa, J.R. Watkins Co., Winona, Minnesota, 5.5"; A&P Cocoa, 4.75", paper label; Baker's Cocoa, Dorchester, Massachusetts, 4.25". *Courtesy of Betty Lou and Frank Gay.*

Assorted cocoa tins (l-r): Baker's German's Sweet Chocolate, Dorchester, Massachusetts; Rawleigh's Cocoa, W.T. Rawleigh, Freeport, Illinois; Watkins Cocoa, J.R. Watkins, Winona, Minnesota, 3.5"; Our Mother's Cocoa, E. & A. Opler, Inc., Chicago, 7.25"; Baker's Cocoa, Walter Baker & Co., Inc., Dorchester, 3.25"; Runkel's Cocoa, New York, 6"; Sandow's Cocoa, Ltd, London, 3.25". *Courtesy of John & Elsie Booker, Patterson's Mill Country Store, Chapel Hill.*

A beautiful self-framing tin sign for Runkel Brothers Cocoa and Chocolates. Charles W. Shonk Co., New York, copyright 1904. 28" x 22". *Courtesy of Betty Lou and Frank Gay.*

Wan-Eta Cocoa jar, Boston. Amber glass, 7" x 4". *Courtesy of Koehler Bros. Inc.—The General Store, Lafayette, Indiana.*

Two Runkel Brothers Cocoa tins. The one on the left is smooth, while the right hand one is embossed. Lithographed tin. *Courtesy of Koehler Bros. Inc.—The General Store, Lafayette, Indiana.*

COFFEE AND TEA

COFFEE GRINDERS

Small tin, wood, and iron coffee mill, 7.5" x 4". *Courtesy of Koehler Bros. Inc.—The General Store, Lafayette, Indiana.*

Oak and cast iron coffee mill with dovetailed cabinetry. This was a portable mill that was held in place by sitting on the long extension of wood. This was also used to hang it to the wall. 10" x 21". *Courtesy of Koehler Bros. Inc.—The General Store, Lafayette, Indiana.*

Colonial Coffee Mill, no. 1707, manufactured by Wrightville Hardware Company. Cast iron and wood, 10" x 6" x 6". *Courtesy of the Mast General Store, Valle Crucis, North Carolina.*

Landers, Frary, and Clark cast iron coffee mill, 11.5" x 5" x 5". *Courtesy of Koehler Bros. Inc.—The General Store, Lafayette, Indiana.*

Tin Crown Coffee Mill, Landers, Frary, & Clark, New Britain, Connecticut. 8" x 6" x 6". *Courtesy of Koehler Bros. Inc.--The General Store, Lafayette, Indiana.*

Floor model coffee grinder designed to run on from a motor via a belt drive. *Courtesy of Koehler Bros. Inc.—The General Store, Lafayette, Indiana.*

A larger Landers, Frary, and Clark coffee mill, 25″ x 9″ x 9″.
*Courtesy of Koehler Bros. Inc.—The General Store,
Lafayette, Indiana.*

Cast iron Grand Union Grinder. 9″ x 5″. *Courtesy of Koehler Bros. Inc.—The General Store, Lafayette, Indiana.*

Small Enterprise coffee mill, Enterprise, Philadelphia, Pennsylvania. Cast iron, 13″ x 11″ x 10″. *Courtesy of Koehler Bros. Inc.—The General Store, Lafayette, Indiana.*

Counter top coffee grinder by Enterprise, Philadelphia. Cast Iron, 24″ x 17″ x 13″. *Courtesy of Koehler Bros. Inc.—The General Store, Lafayette, Indiana.*

Wood and cast iron Telephone Grinder, designed to be hung on the wall. 13″ x 8″ x 5″. *Courtesy of Koehler Bros. Inc.—The General Store, Lafayette, Indiana.*

Wooden A & P Coffee bin with transfer decorations, 30.5" x 18" x 18". *Courtesy of Koehler Bros. Inc.—The General Store, Lafayette, Indiana.*

Amazon Coffee Bin, wood with stenciled letters. 31" x 21" x 16". *Courtesy of Koehler Bros. Inc.—The General Store, Lafayette, Indiana.*

One pound paper packages of Arbuckles' Ariosa Coffee, Arbuckle Brothers, New York. 4" x 7". *Courtesy of Betty Lou and Frank Gay.*

Two Bokar Coffee tins. The older one on the left is 5" tall, while the other is 5.75". This was a brand of the Great Atlantic & Pacific (A & P) Tea Company, New York. *Courtesy of John & Elsie Booker, Patterson's Mill Country Store, Chapel Hill.*

Rare Brownie Coffee tin with paper label. Stokes Coffee Co., Baltimore, Maryland, 6″ x 4.5″ x 3″. *Courtesy of John & Elsie Booker, Patterson's Mill Country Store, Chapel Hill.*

Wooden shipping crate for Chase & Sanborn Seal Brand Coffee. 10″ x 10″ x 24″. *Courtesy of the Mast General Store, Valle Crucis, North Carolina.*

Wood and paper coffee barrel for Our Breakfast Coffee, Reid, Murdoch & Co., Chicago and New York. 34″ x 22″. *Courtesy of Koehler Bros. Inc.—The General Store, Lafayette, Indiana.*

5″ cloth mammy doll for Crystal Coffee. This is typical of dolls made from kits that were given as premiums, though one cannot be sure. *Courtesy of Koehler Bros. Inc.—The General Store, Lafayette, Indiana.*

Well-executed 120 pound Jersey Coffee bin. Stenciled wood, 32″ x 22.5″ x 19.5″. Dayton Spice Mills Co. *Courtesy of Koehler Bros. Inc.—The General Store, Lafayette, Indiana.*

Jar for Hart's Coffee, James E. Hart, Cincinnati, Ohio. 8.25″ x 4″. *Courtesy of Koehler Bros. Inc.— The General Store, Lafayette, Indiana.*

Large cabin-shaped bin for Johnson's Log Cabin Coffee, c. 1912. Lithographed tin, 25" x 24" x 18". *Courtesy of Koehler Bros. Inc.—The General Store, Lafayette, Indiana.*

Kenny's Maid Coffee tin pail, C.D. Kenny Co., Baltimore, Maryland. 8″ tall. *Courtesy of Betty Lou and Frank Gay.*

Three versions of the Mammy's Favorite Brand Coffee 4 pound tins, the C.D. Kenny Co., Baltimore, Maryland. The center tin is the rarest of the three. 11″ tall, 6.25″ in diameter. *Courtesy of Betty Lou and Frank Gay.*

Malden brand coffee tin with paper label. Sears, Roebuck & Co., Chicago, Illinois. 11″ tall. *Courtesy of Betty Lou and Frank Gay.*

Early None-Such coffee grinder. Tin and iron with a wooden drawer. 9″ x 5″ x 5″. *Courtesy of Koehler Bros. Inc.—The General Store, Lafayette, Indiana.*

Later None-Such coffee grinder manufactured by the Mirroscope Co. 11.5″ x 7″ x 7″. *Courtesy of Koehler Bros. Inc.—The General Store, Lafayette, Indiana.*

Beautifully lithographed bin for Number 20 Blend Coffee. It features the Triunfo Plantation of the German-American Coffee Co., New York, Chicago, Des Moines, Omaha. 15.25″ x 21″. *Courtesy of Betty Lou and Frank Gay.*

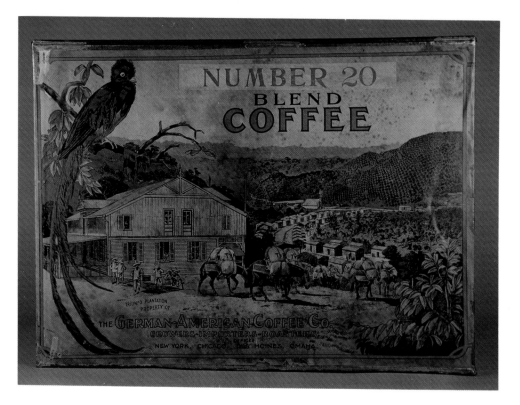

Five pound tin pail for Pilot-Knob Coffee. It features Pilot Mountain in North Carolina. Bowers Brothers, Inc., Richmond, Virginia. 9" x 7.5". *Courtesy of Betty Lou and Frank Gay.*

Grinder advertising Hoffman's "Old Time" Coffee, Milwaukee. 13.5" x 7". *Courtesy of Koehler Bros. Inc.—The General Store, Lafayette, Indiana.*

Three pound tin pail and one pound paper pack of Pilot-Knob Coffee. The pail is 8.25" tall. *Courtesy of John & Elsie Booker, Patterson's Mill Country Store, Chapel Hill.*

Tin bin for Scull's "Grind it as you want it" Coffee. 22" x 20". *Courtesy of Koehler Bros. Inc.—The General Store, Lafayette, Indiana.*

Opposite page top:
Assorted coffee tins (l-r): Boston Blend, 6"; Arbuckles' Breakfast Coffee, 6.5"; Autocrat Coffee, Brownell & Field Co., Providence, Rhode Island, 5"; Miss Carolina Coffee, Carolina Coffee Co., Charleston, South Carolina, 3.5" x 5"; Old Mansion Coffee, Richmond, Virginia. *Courtesy of John & Elsie Booker, Patterson's Mill Country Store, Chapel Hill.*

Opposite page bottom:
Assorted coffee tins (l-r): Ponce de Leon Coffee, Humphrey & Cornell, Providence, Rhode Island, 4" x 6"; Momaja Coffee, Keys, Corsa, & Holley, New York, 7" x 3.75", American Can Co.; Bouquet Coffee, O.V. Tracey, Syracuse, New York, 6.75" x 4.5", American Can Co.; Rose Bud Coffee, Walrath & Manz, Syracuse, New York, 4" x 6"; Elephant Java Coffee, Jos. Stiner & Co., New York, 5" x 7.5". *Courtesy of Betty Lou and Frank Gay.*

Wood coffee bin for Steer Brand Tip Top Roasted Coffee. Roth-Homeyer Coffee Co., St. Louis, Missouri, 31.5" x 23" x 16". *Courtesy of Koehler Bros. Inc.—The General Store, Lafayette, Indiana.*

Two tins from major department stores. Left: Five pound Rivera Brand Coffee tin, Sears, Roebuck, & Co., Chicago, 12" x 7". Right: Java and Arabian Mocha Coffee tin, Montgomery Ward & Co., New York, 10" x 7". *Courtesy of Betty Lou and Frank Gay.*

Opposite page top:

Assorted one pound coffee tins, 6" tall. Top row (l-r) Gladiator Club Coffee, B.C. & Co., paper label; Berma Coffee, Grand Union Company, New York; Larkin 55 cent Blend Coffee, Larkin Co., Buffalo, paper label; Excelsior Coffee, Dwinell-Wright Co., Boston-Chicago, paper label. Bottom row (l-r): Acme Coffee, American Stores Co., Philadelphia; New & True Coffee, Binghamton, New York, paper label lithographed by Stecher Litho, Rochester; Otsega Coffee, Oneonta Grocery Co., Oneonta, New York, paper label; Mother's Joy Coffee, American Stores Co., Philadelphia. *Courtesy of Betty Lou and Frank Gay.*

Opposite page bottom:

Assorted one pound coffee tins, 6" tall. Top row (l-r): Lipton's Yellow Label Brand Coffee, c. 1920; ENERGY Coffee, Behring-Stahl Coffee Co., St. Louis, Missouri; Veteran Coffee, Brewster Gordon & Co., Rochester, American Can Co.; Matchless Coffee, Charles E. Moody & Co., Boston, c. 1923. Bottom row (l-r): Almoco Coffee, Levering Coffee Co., Baltimore, paper label; Eagle Coffee, Eagle Grocery Co., Jersey City, New Jersey; Old Master Coffee, Toledo, Ohio; Boscul Coffee, William S. Scull Co., paper label. *Courtesy of Betty Lou and Frank Gay.*

Assorted one pound coffee tins, 6" tall. Top row (l-r): Reception Java & Mocha Coffee, Oriental Coffee Co., New York; Freshpak Coffee, Grand Union Company, New York; Steel Cut Coffee, paper label; Royal Luncheon Coffee, paper label. Bottom row (l-r): Union Club Coffee, Chas. G. Lincoln & Company, Hartford Connecticut; Superba Coffee, Milliken-Tomlinson Co., Portland, Maine; Seal Brand Coffee, Chase and Sanborn Co., Boston; Yellow Gold Coffee, C.D. Kenny Co., 1937. paper label. *Courtesy of Betty Lou and Frank Gay.*

Assorted coffee tins. Top row (l-r): Knobbed coffee tin, Thos. Wood & Co., Boston, 6.5″; L.H. Parke's Newport Coffee, Pittsburgh, 6″; American Ace Coffee, American Tea & Coffee Co., Nashville, Tennessee, 5″; Luzianne white lithographed tin, Wm. B. Reilly & Company, New Orleans, 6″. Bottom row (l-r): Chase and Sanborn Coffee, copyright 1932 by Standards Inc., New York, 6″; White House Coffee, Dwinell-Wright Company, paper label; Breakfast Cheer Coffee, the Campbell Woods Co., Pittsburgh; Luzianne Coffee, paper label, Wm. B. Reilly & Company, New Orleans, 6″.

TEA

"In Trouble." An 1884 stand-up advertising piece for the Great Atlantic & Pacific Tea Company. Paper, 9″ x 5.5″. *Courtesy of Betty Lou and Frank Gay.*

Stoneware tea pot for Blanke's Tea. 6.5" x 8". *Courtesy of Koehler Bros. Inc.—The General Store, Lafayette, Indiana.*

Two round tins for the McCormick Banquet Teas, Baltimore, Maryland. Top: 1.5" x 3.25"; bottom: 2" x 4". *Courtesy of Betty Lou and Frank Gay.*

A collection of McCormick Banquet Tea tins, and a bag with the label in the form of a tin. McCormick & Co., Baltimore. *Courtesy of John & Elsie Booker, Patterson's Mill Country Store, Chapel Hill.*

Monarch Tea tins, Reid, Murdock & Co., Chicago & New York, 4.25" & 5.5" tall. *Courtesy of John & Elsie Booker, Patterson's Mill Country Store, Chapel Hill.*

Tea tins (l-r): Maxwell House Tea, Cheek-Neal Coffee Co., 4.75"; Elephant Compound, Potter, Sloan, O'Donahue Co., Brooklyn, 5.25", paper label; Old Fire Side Tea, Swain Earle & Co., Boston, Massachusetts, 4.5"; Betsy Ross Tea, Plunkett-Jarrell Grocer Co., Little Rock, Arkansas. *Courtesy of John & Elsie Booker, Patterson's Mill Country Store, Chapel Hill.*

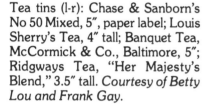

Tea tins (l-r): Chase & Sanborn's No 50 Mixed, 5", paper label; Louis Sherry's Tea, 4" tall; Banquet Tea, McCormick & Co., Baltimore, 5"; Ridgways Tea, "Her Majesty's Blend," 3.5" tall. *Courtesy of Betty Lou and Frank Gay.*

Tack Kee & Co.'s Jasmine Tea tin, Hong Kong. Ting Hing Wo Can Mfg., paper label, 5" x 4.5" x 2.5". *Courtesy of Koehler Bros. Inc.— The General Store, Lafayette, Indiana.*

Cardboard sign for Richelieu Brand Teas, Sprague Warner & Co., Chicago, c. 1916. 11.5" x 21". *Courtesy of Koehler Bros. Inc.—The General Store, Lafayette, Indiana.*

Assorted tea containers, (l-r): Richelieu Tea Balls, Sprague, Warner & Co., Chicago, 6"; Grandmother's Tea, Great Atlantic & Pacific Tea Co., 3.75"; Maxwell House Tea, General Foods, New York, 3.5"; White Rose Tea Balls, Seeman Bros., New York; 10"; Perri-Walla Tea, Francis H. Leggett & Co., New York, 3.25"; Lipton's Tea, London; Tetley's Tea, 3.75", with a tea bag. *Courtesy of John & Elsie Booker, Patterson's Mill Country Store, Chapel Hill.*

Tea tins (l-r): Golden Dome Tea, W.S. Quinby Co., Boston-Chicago, 8" including the Massachusetts State House Dome; Maxwell House Blend, Cheek-Neal Coffee Co., 4"; Ambero Tea, Berry, Dodge Co., Boston-Newburyport, Massachusetts, 4.25"; None Such Brand Tea, McNeil & Higgins Co., Chicago, 4.25". *Courtesy of Betty Lou and Frank Gay.*

DAIRY PRODUCTS AND EGGS

Wooden Borden's Farm Products display/toy.
13.5" x 29". Courtesy of Koehler Bros. Inc.—
The General Store, Lafayette, Indiana.

Kraft Cheese stand. Wood, 13" x 15" x 3".
Courtesy of Koehler Bros. Inc.—The General
Store, Lafayette, Indiana.

Crate for Shefford Cream Cheese, Shefford Cheese Co., Syracuse-Green Bay. *Courtesy of John & Elsie Booker, Patterson's Mill Country Store, Chapel Hill.*

Aluminum egg box used for mailing eggs. Patented in 1920 by Metal Products Co., Fredericksburg, Virginia. 6″ x 13″ x 9.5″ *Courtesy of John & Elsie Booker, Patterson's Mill Country Store, Chapel Hill.*

Star Egg Carriers, c. 1910. John Elbs, Rochester, New York, 3″ x 8.25″ x 12.5″. *Courtesy of John & Elsie Booker, Patterson's Mill Country Store, Chapel Hill.*

Wood egg crate with sliding top and pressed cardboard separators. 12″ x 13″ x 13″. *Courtesy of John & Elsie Booker, Patterson's Mill Country Store, Chapel Hill.*

LARD AND SHORTENING

Cardboard counter stand for Crisco shortening, with changeable pricing. Proctor & Gamble Co., Cincinnati, Ohio. 5" x 8". The tin has a paper label and measures 3.5" x 4". *Courtesy of Betty Lou and Frank Gay.*

Tin pail for Proctor & Gamble's Flakewhite lard made at Ivorydale, Ohio. *Courtesy of John & Elsie Booker, Patterson's Mill Country Store, Chapel Hill.*

Two tins for Ensign Brand lard, C.G. Kriel Co., Baltimore. One, 11", is 25 pound; the other, 5.5", is three pounds. The tin on the right is marked Platt Can Company. *Courtesy of Betty Lou and Frank Gay.*

Tin for H.G. Sense's Strictly Pure Lard, Lafayette, Indiana. *Courtesy of Koehler Bros. Inc.—The General Store, Lafayette, Indiana.*

50 pound tin for Victory lard, Chas. Sucher Packing, Dayton, Ohio. 15″ x 12″. *Courtesy of John & Elsie Booker, Patterson's Mill Country Store, Chapel Hill.*

Various 4 pound lard pails. Top (l-r) Whiteleaf Brand, Morris & Co., Chicago; Piedmont Quality, Piedmont Packing, Hillsboro, North Carolina; Luter's Pure Lard, Smithfield Packing, Smithfield, Virginia. Bottom (l-r): Dixie's Unexcelled Brand, Hickory Packing, Hickory, North Carolina; Kingan's Reliable, Kingan & Co., Indianapolis; White Seal, White Packing Co., Salisbury, North Carolina; White Pure Lard, White Packing Co. *Courtesy of John & Elsie Booker, Patterson's Mill Country Store, Chapel Hill.*

Various 4 pound lard pails. Top (l-r): Snowdrift Shortening, Wesson Oil and Snowdrift Sales Co., New Orleans; White Compound, "Cudahy of Cudahy," Wisconsin; Swift's Jewel, Swift & Company. Bottom (l-r): Swift's Jewel Shortening, Swift & Company; Hormel Minnesota Pure Lard, Geo. A. Hormel & Co., Austin, Minnesota; Hormel Pure Lard, Geo. A. Hormel & Co.; Swift's Silver Leaf Brand Lard, Swift & Company. *Courtesy of Koehler Bros. Inc.—The General Store, Lafayette, Indiana.*

SPICES

An octagonal tin caddy featuring lithography of the highest quality. Each of the main panels has a scene from a different country. Keen's Mustard, England, 6" x 8". *Courtesy of Betty Lou and Frank Gay.*

Spice tin for Golden Sun Tumeric, a product of the Woolson Spice Co., Toledo, c. 1912. The tin was made by Passaic Metal Ware Co., Passaic, New Jersey. 3.5″ x 2.25″ x 1.25″. *Courtesy of Koehler Bros. Inc.—The General Store, Lafayette, Indiana.*

Galvanized pail for Senator brand pepper, Chas. King & Son Co., Inc., Charlottesville and Alexandria, Virginia. 14″ x 13.5″. *Courtesy of Betty Lou and Frank Gay.*

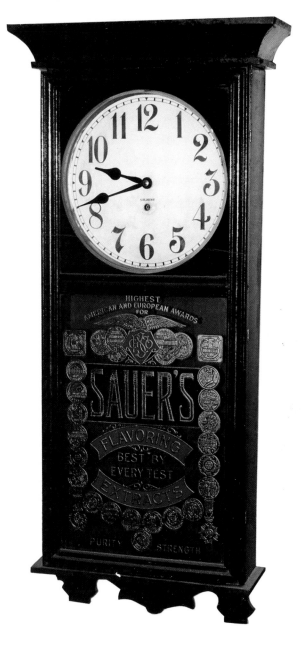

A Gilbert key wound pendulum clock advertising Sauer's flavorings and extracts on its gilded glass panel. *Courtesy of Betty Lou and Frank Gay.*

Ginger tins. Top left: White Rose Ginger, Seeman Brothers, New York, 1″ x 4″. Bottom left: Rich's Crystallized Canton Ginger, E.C. Rich, Inc., New York; 2″ x 6″. Right: Crystallized Ginger, Sunbeam Pure Food, Nichols & Co., Inc., New York, 2″ x 6″. *Courtesy of John and Elsie Booker, Patterson's Mill Country Store, Chapel Hill.*

Assorted spice containers. Top: Hatchet Brand Whole Cloves, The Twitchell Champlin Co., Portland, Maine, 3.5″ wide, cardboard. Bottom (l-r): Full Dress Spices, James G. Gill Co., Norfolk, Virginia, 3.5″; Hudson Brand Allspice, 3.5″; Dove Brand Rubbed Sage, The Frank Tea & Spice Co., Cincinnati, Ohio, 3.75″; Rajah Paprika, The Great Atlantic and Pacific Tea Company, New York, 3″. *Courtesy of Betty Lou and Frank Gay.*

A wooden Sauer's thermometer in the shape of a box of vanilla, c. 1920. *Courtesy of Betty Lou and Frank Gay.*

Left: Two spice tins from James P. Smith & Co., New York, 3.75", the American Can Company. Center: A pepper tin from the Great American Tea Company, New York, 4". Right: Four tins from A & P. *Courtesy of Betty Lou and Frank Gay.*

One of a set of spice bins by the S.A. Isley Can Co., New York. This one is 12" x 8". *Courtesy of Betty Lou and Frank Gay.*

Tin and glass case for Freihofer's Quality Cakes, 22" x 15" x 15". *Courtesy of Koehler Bros. Inc.—The General Store, Lafayette, Indiana.*

Small oaken barrel for California Sweet Pickled Figs, H. Jeyne Co., 9″ x 7″. *Courtesy of John & Elsie Booker, Patterson's Mill Country Store, Chapel Hill.*

Tins for coconut. Top: Baker's Coconut, General Foods, 9″ tall; right: Snowdrift Coconut, Franklin Baker Co., Hoboken, New Jersey, 6/75″. *Courtesy of John & Elsie Booker, Patterson's Mill Country Store, Chapel Hill.*

Ten pound tin with paper label for Monarch Cream, Monarch Chemical, New York, 10″ x 6.75″. *Courtesy of Koehler Bros. Inc.—The General Store, Lafayette, Indiana.*

Wesson Oil mayonnaise maker. The recipe was: 1 egg; 2 tablespoons lemon juice or vinegar; 1 teaspoon each of mustard, salt, and sugar; a dash of pepper; and one pint Wesson Oil. Beat thoroughly. Glass and metal, 13″ x 3.5″. *Courtesy of Betty Lou and Frank Gay.*

Two oak bucket containers. Left: Atmore's Celebrated Mince Meat, Atmore & Son Co., Philadelphia, 8″ x 8″. Right: Heinz Pickles, 10″ x 9″. *Courtesy of Koehler Bros. Inc.—The General Store, Lafayette, Indiana.*

Marshmallow tins (top to bottom): Melrose Marshmallows, Emma A. Curtis, Melrose, Massachusetts, 4.25″ x 2″; Campfire Marshmallows, the Campfire Company, Milwaukee, 5.5″ x 3.5″, paper label; Melrose Marshmallows, 9.5″ x 6″; Unicy (U-and-I-C-why) Marshmallows, Bradle & Smith Co., Philadelphia, 9.5″ x 6″, Liberty Can Co., Lancaster, Pennsylvania. *Courtesy of Betty Lou and Frank Gay.*

Molasses and syrup containers (l-r): Sho' Is Fine Syrup, Penick & Ford Ltd, New Orleans, 6.75″; Monogram Syrup, Imperial Coffee Co., Richmond, 5.75″; Golden Rule Molasses, Citizens Wholesale Supply Company, Columbus, Ohio, 11″; Brer Rabbit Molasses, Penick & Ford Ltd., New Orleans, 6.75″; Vermont Maid Syrup, Vermont Maid Maple Syrup Co., Burlington, Vermont, 5.5″. *Courtesy of John & Elsie Booker, Patterson's Mill Country Store, Chapel Hill.*

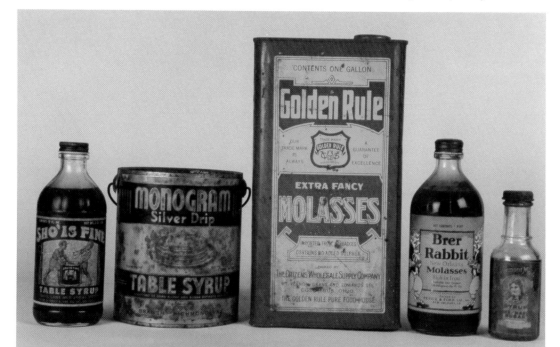

Covington Molasses 5 gallon tin, American Molasses of North Carolina, Wilmington, North Carolina, 13″ x 11″. *Courtesy of John & Elsie Booker, Patterson's Mill Country Store, Chapel Hill.*

Oyster pail, Louis Grebb, packer, Baltimore, Maryland. 7.25″ x 7″. *Courtesy of Betty Lou and Frank Gay.*

Oysters were a great delicacy and a very popular product on country store shelves, especially around the holidays. Left to right: Stag Brand, Planters Packing Co.; Sun Brand, the Leib Packing Co., tin made by Atlantic Can Co., Baltimore; Arrow Brand, J.J. Lansburgh & Co. All three tins were packed in Baltimore, the center of the oyster industry, and measure 7″ x 3.5″. *Courtesy of Betty Lou and Frank Gay.*

Chapter Three

Sweets and Treats

ICE CREAM AND CANDY

Eskimo Pie thermos with cast eskimos as the feet. Louisville, Kentucky, 15". *Courtesy of Betty Lou and Frank Gay.*

Sidewalk sign for Ice Cream and Cold Drinks. Wood and tin, 34" x 22". *Courtesy of Koehler Bros. Inc. — The General Store, Lafayette, Indiana.*

To keep ice cream frozen on its way home from the store, it was packed in ingenious containers like this one for High's sherbet. The container is by Thermopak, New York and is of paper. *Courtesy of Betty Lou and Frank Gay.*

This tin display for Frozen Powerhouse Candy Bars makes a nice transition from ice cream to candy. This old idea has come back, as several candy bar manufacturers are offering their wares in frozen form. 9" x 15" x 8". *Courtesy of Koehler Bros. Inc.—The General Store, Lafayette, Indiana.*

No country store would be complete without a wide selection of candy. Here are some original packages from Todd General Store. *Courtesy of the Todd General Store, Todd, North Carolina.*

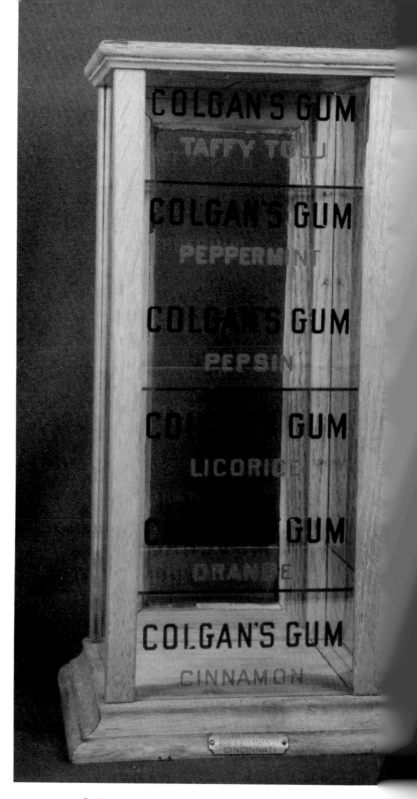

Coin-operated machine offering samples of Adam's Pepsin gum for one cent. Wood and glass, marked "A.S. Co. of Am." on the lock. 30.5" tall. *Courtesy of Betty Lou and Frank Gay.*

Oak and glass case for Colgan's Gum. Schmitt & Cincinnati, Ohio, 17.5" x 9" x 8". *Courtesy of Gary N Roanoke, Virginia.*

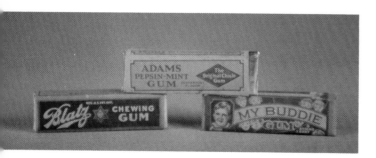

Chewing gum packs (l-r): Blatz Chewing Gum, Blatz Co., Chicago; Adams Pepsin-Mint Gum, American C Company; My Buddie Gum, L.P. Larson, Jr., Comp Newport, Rhode Island. *Courtesy of Betty Lou and F Gay.*

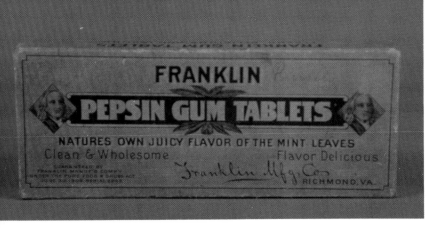

Box for Franklin's Pepsin Gum Tablets, Franklin Mfg. Co., Richmond, Virginia, c. 1910. Cardboard, 3.5″ x 9″ x 1″. *Courtesy of Betty Lou and Frank Gay.*

Three tins for Necco Peach Blossoms, New England Confectionary Co. The one on the left is marked Boston, the one on the right, Cambridge, and the center tin was manufactured by the Colonial Can Company, Boston. 9″ tall. *Courtesy of John & Elsie Booker, Patterson's Mill Country Store, Chapel Hill.*

Walnut and glass case for Jones' gums: Columbian Fruit, Tuxedo, and Pepsin-Phosphate. 7″ x 17.5″ x 9.5″. *Courtesy of Koehler Bros. Inc.—The General Store, Lafayette, Indiana.*

Self-framing tin sign for Nobility Chocolates. H.D. Beach Co., Coshocton, Ohio, c. 1900. 22.5″ x 28.5″. *Courtesy of Koehler Bros. Inc.—The General Store, Lafayette, Indiana.*

Wrigley's gum packs. The packs with the NRA logo are circa 1933. The PK Peppermint pack is copyrighted 1921. *Courtesy of Betty Lou and Frank Gay.*

Tin Wrigley's truck display/toy. 9.5″ x 23.5″. The head lights work on batteries. *Courtesy of Koehler Bros. Inc.—The General Store, Lafayette, Indiana.*

PEANUTS AND PEANUT BUTTER

BeeBee's Salted shell peanut warmer and display. Tin and glass, 21" tall. *Courtesy of Betty Lou and Frank Gay.*

What could be better than hot peanuts from the Acme Peanut Roaster? Tin, 24" x 18" x 18". Mattapoisett, Massachusetts, c. 1895. *Courtesy of Koehler Bros. Inc.— The General Store, Lafayette, Indiana.*

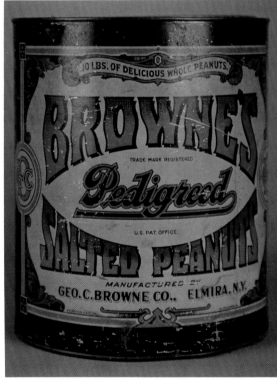

Two Allen & Smith Co. products. On the left is Dad's Favorite Goober Nuts and on the right is Goodnuff Salted Peanuts. Both tins are 10" x 8.5". *Courtesy of Betty Lou and Frank Gay.*

10 pound tin for Browne's Pedigreed Salted Peanuts, Geo. C. Browne Co., Elmira, New York. The tin is 9.75" x 8.25" and was manufactured by W.B. Bertels & Son Co., Wilkes-Barre, Pennsylvania. *Courtesy of Betty Lou and Frank Gay.*

Tin for Buffalo Brand peanuts, E.M. Hoyt & Co., Amesbury, Massachusetts. The tin was manufactured by Southern Can Co., Baltimore, Maryland. On the top are directions for keeping the contents fresh and another nicely rendered litho of the Buffalo Brand logo. *Courtesy of Betty Lou and Frank Gay.*

Counter jar for Curtiss Chicos Spanish Peanuts. Glass and tin, 11″ x 8″ x 8″. *Courtesy of Koehler Bros. Inc.—The General Store, Lafayette, Indiana.*

Crispaco Salted Peanuts 10 pound tin, Crisp Packing Co., Petersburg, Virginia. The tin was manufactured by Southern Can Co., Baltimore, Maryland.

Eastern Brand Salted Peanuts, Eastern Peanut Company, Hereford, North Carolina. The tin is by W.B. Bertels & Son, Wilkes-Barre, Pennsylvania. *Courtesy of Betty Lou and Frank Gay.*

Ten pound tin for Giant Peanuts, the Superior Peanut Company, Cleveland, Ohio. *Courtesy of Betty Lou and Frank Gay.*

Display shelf for the Nut House. Tin, 24″ x 17″ x 7″. *Courtesy of Koehler Bros. Inc.—The General Store, Lafayette, Indiana.*

Ten pound tin for Mammoth Brand Salted Peanuts. The Kelly Co., Cleveland, Ohio. 11″ tall. *Courtesy of Betty Lou and Frank Gay.*

Ten, five, and one pound tins for Picnic Peanuts, Producers Peanut Co., Suffolk, Virginia. Heights are 9.75″, 7.75″, and 3.25″, respectively. *Courtesy of Betty Lou and Frank Gay.*

Robinson Crusoe tins from the H.A. Robinson Co., Inc., Lynchburg, Virginia. The tin on the left is a classic, but not as rare as the tin on the right. *Courtesy of Betty Lou and Frank Gay.*

Left: Mosemann's Peanut butter tin pail, Mosemann Co., Lancaster, Pennsylvania, 7" tall. Right: Mewhinney's Peanut Butter tin, Terre Haute, Indiana, 5.5" tall. *Courtesy of John & Elsie Booker, Patterson's Mill Country Store, Chapel Hill.*

Triangle Club Peanut Butter tin pail, Montgomery Ward & Co., New York. *Courtesy of Betty Lou and Frank Gay.*

One pound tin of Long's Ox-Heart Brand Peanut Butter, Oswego Candy Co., Oswego, New York. The tin is 3.5" x 3.5" and was manufactured by CANCO. *Courtesy of Koehler Bros. Inc.—The General Store, Lafayette, Indiana.*

SOFT DRINKS

Next to the potbellied stove and the porch, the most important social feature of the country store may have been the Coca-Cola cooler. This one still gathers a crowd at the Mast Store. 35" x 70". *Courtesy of the Mast General Store, Valle Crucis, North Carolina.*

Anytime is time for a Coke. Key wound pendulum advertising clock. *Courtesy of Betty Lou and Frank Gay.*

Wood Coca-Cola thermometer. 20". *Courtesy of Betty Lou and Frank Gay.*

Dry-Server bag to go over your Coke bottle. D.J. Renfroe Corporation, Thomasville, Georgia. 6". *Courtesy of Betty Lou and Frank Gay.*

Coca-Cola paper bag holder. Tin, 17" x 37". *Courtesy of Betty Lou and Frank Gay.*

Aluminum Coke carriers for six bottles. *Courtesy of John & Elsie Booker, Patterson's Mill Country Store, Chapel Hill.*

Steel railroad crate for carrying three cases of Coca-Cola. Coca-Cola is embossed on the top and sides. Danville, Virginia, 9.25" x 32" x 16". *Courtesy of John & Elsie Booker, Patterson's Mill Country Store, Chapel Hill.*

Aluminum carrier for Diet-Rite Cola, c. 1960. *Courtesy of the Mast General Store, Valle Crucis, North Carolina.*

Glass Dr. Pepper sign, 15" x 23". *Courtesy of Koehler Bros. Inc.—The General Store, Lafayette, Indiana.*

Pepsi carriers. *Courtesy of John & Elsie Booker, Patterson's Mill Country Store, Chapel Hill.*

Tin drums for Pepsi syrup. 17" x 16". *Courtesy of Betty Lou and Frank Gay.*

A Pepsi cooler from a Durham baseball park. It is designed to be used in two ways. With the cooler set in the frame it can be carried into the baseball bleachers. Turn the frame over and it is a convenient Pepsi stand. 13.5" x 27". *Courtesy of Betty Lou and Frank Gay.*

Embossed tin sign for Pepsi'Cola and the Bon-Ton Country Store, c. 1920s. *Courtesy of Betty Lou and Frank Gay.*

Carriers for TruAde, 7-up, and Royal Crown Cola. 9.5″-10″ tall. *Courtesy of John & Elsie Booker, Patterson's Mill Country Store, Chapel Hill.*

Fountain bottle for Allen's Red Tame Cherry "Cherryallen" syrup. Glass with recessed reverse painted glass label, 11″ tall. *Courtesy of Koehler Bros. Inc.—The General Store, Lafayette, Indiana.*

Chapter Four

Smokes and Spirits

TOBACCO

This hanging barrel sign for Allen & Ginter Richmond Straight Cut No. 1 Cigarette Leaf Tobacco, features actual tobacco leaves behind reverse painted and gilded glass. 14″ in diameter. *Courtesy of Betty Lou and Frank Gay.*

Wooden cigar store Indian, c. 1920s, 74″ tall. *Courtesy of Koehler Bros. Inc.—The General Store, Lafayette, Indiana.*

Cigar cutter advertising John Anderson & Co.'s "Extra" fine cut chewing tobacco, "The Best in the World for 5 cents." Cast iron, 19". *Courtesy of Betty Lou and Frank Gay.*

Cast iron cigar cutter advertising Artie Cigars, "The Best of the Year." A guillotine action nipped the cigar when it was inserted in the hole. 10" tall. *Courtesy of Betty Lou and Frank Gay.*

Cardboard sign for Barking Dog cigarettes, by Philip Morris. 26″ x 13″. *Courtesy of Betty Lou and Frank Gay.*

Only known poster for Brotherhood Cut Plug Tobacco. Living up to its name, the text is an announcement that Brotherhood Cut Plug Tobacco coupons may be redeemed for the purchase of artificial arms and legs for those "unfortunate as to lose their's." As a starter they offer 500 free coupons to anyone who has lost an arm and 1000 coupons to anyone who has lost a leg. Paper, 24.25″ x 16″. *Courtesy of John & Elsie Booker, Patterson's Mill Country Store, Chapel Hill.*

Rare early checkerboard for W.T. Blackwell's Genuine Durham Smoking Tobacco. Cardboard, 20″ x 30″. *Courtesy of Betty Lou and Frank Gay.*

Front of W.T. Blackwell's checker-board.

After World War I, it became more acceptable for women to smoke cigarettes. In 1932 this Bull Durham advertisement appeared showing what Thomas Clark called a "dreamy-eyed matronly jersey" looking lovingly at "her hero" on the billboard. A rare poster in excellent condition, 23″ x 18″, it carries and acknowledgement to John Held, Jr. *Courtesy of John & Elsie Booker, Patterson's Mill Country Store, Chapel Hill.*

Tin chest with locking clasp, for Buck Cigars, "King of the Range." 18″ x 27″ x 18″. *Courtesy of Koehler Bros. Inc.— The General Store, Lafayette, Indiana.*

Tin and glass counter case for Eisenlohr's Cinco cigars. 14″ x 9″ x 15″. *Courtesy of Koehler Bros. Inc.—The General Store, Lafayette, Indiana.*

Tin dispenser for Diamond matches. 13″ tall. *Courtesy of Betty Lou and Frank Gay.*

Tin counter box for Cremo Cigars. 6″ x 14″ x 6″. *Courtesy of Koehler Bros. Inc.—The General Store, Lafayette, Indiana.*

Duke's Cameo chair. Wood with paper label. 30″ tall. *Courtesy of Koehler Bros. Inc.—The General Store, Lafayette, Indiana.*

Paper poster featuring the Musical Instruments series of Duke cigarette cards. 27.5″ x 13″. *Courtesy of Betty Lou and Frank Gay.*

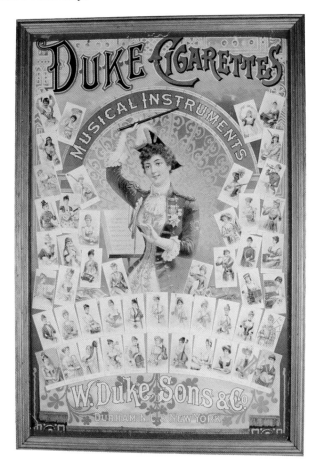

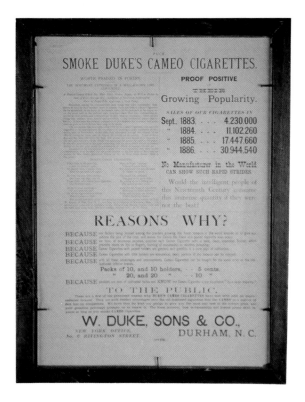

Poster for Duke's Cameo cigarettes, a brand that came with a little holder. The front has President Cleveland suggesting to the Secretary of State that Cameo Cigarettes be sent to Mexico as a compromise in the event of further problems. The back documents the growth of Duke cigarettes in the years leading up to 1886. *Courtesy of Betty Lou and Frank Gay.*

Duke's Mixture fan which reads "A delightfully cool smoke." 8.5". *Courtesy of Betty Lou and Frank Gay.*

Front and back views of a nicely done Duke's Cameo cigarettes chair. 33" tall. *Courtesy of Betty Lou and Frank Gay.*

A sepia-toned photograph of a woman smoking Duke's Preferred Stock Cigarettes adorns this cardboard sign. While it may be all right for this scantily clad woman to smoke cigarettes, it is doubtful that any man at the turn of the century would want his wife to do so. 10.75" x 6.75". *Courtesy of Betty Lou and Frank Gay.*

Though it has seen a little wear, this rare cardboard sign for Egyptienne Luxury Cigarettes shows the lithographer's art. 27″ x 19.5″. Courtesy of Betty Lou and Frank Gay.

Self-framing tin sign for El Macco Cigars. 24″ x 20″. Courtesy of Koehler Bros. Inc.—The General Store, Lafayette, Indiana.

Nicely designed cardboard poster for Fatima Cigarettes. Liggett & Myers Tobacco Co., c. 1945. 34″ x 20.75″. Courtesy of John & Elsie Booker, Patterson's Mill Country Store, Chapel Hill.

Unable to pass up a successful advertising gimmick, Full Dress brand spices by James G. Gill Co., Norfolk, Virginia borrowed freely from Sears, Roebuck and Co.'s Full Dress tobacco name and logo. Both are very similar to the image on the popular Tuxedo brand tobacco. The spice is 3.5″ tall, and the tobacco is 5″ tall. Courtesy of Betty Lou and Frank Gay.

Cloth and paper package for Hambone Tobacco, J.H. Cosby & Bro., Danville, Virginia. 3.5". *Courtesy of Betty Lou and Frank Gay.*

While smoking or chewing tobacco was taboo for women until after World War I, dipping snuff was quite acceptable, at least in the South. Garrett was one of the earliest and most popular brands on the country store shelf. A paper poster honoring the 150th anniversary of W.E. Garrett & Sons, 1932. 18" x 15". *Courtesy of Betty Lou and Frank Gay.*

Tin and wood display shelf for La Fendrich cigars. 22" x 24". *Courtesy of Koehler Bros. Inc.—The General Store, Lafayette, Indiana.*

Rare cardboard box of The Grand Duchess tobacco, "D'ici le Tabac de Mon Pere!" ("Here is the tobacco of my father!"). Part of the series of 1879 it is 6.5" x 4.25" and features lovely color lithography. *Courtesy of Betty Lou and Frank Gay.*

This rare tin sign for Z.I. Lyon's Pride of Durham Tobacco reveals its beauty despite some serious flaking. Manufactured by Metallic Advertising Signs, Philadelphia. *Courtesy of Betty Lou and Frank Gay.*

Lorillard's Tin Tag Plug Tobacco display case, walnut and glass with brass hardware. 38" x 31" x 17". *Courtesy of Koehler Bros. Inc.—The General Store, Lafayette, Indiana.*

Jar for Mercantile Cigars, Detroit, Michigan. Jar marked: "'Hum Jar,' Factory 155, Dist. of Ohio. 6.5" x 5.5". *Courtesy of Koehler Bros. Inc.—The General Store, Lafayette, Indiana.*

One of a series of Mail Pouch Tobacco cardboard signs, created by artist J. Rozen and published by Carl Percy Inc., New York. 34" x 21". *Courtesy of Koehler Bros. Inc.—The General Store, Lafayette, Indiana.*

These cherubs herald Marburg Brother's Pickings of the Virginia Crop. Cardboard, circa 1890. 8.5" x 12". *Courtesy of Betty Lou and Frank Gay.*

A collection of Niggerhair and Biggerhair Tobacco containers. The name was changed in 1927 with changing sensibilities. Manufactured by B. Leidersdorf Co., Milwaukee, Wisconsin, The American Tobacco Co. *Courtesy of Betty Lou and Frank Gay.*

1860 Old Virginia Smoke tin, Hask & Marcuse Mfg., Richmond. W.T. Hancock, Richmond. 3.75″ x 4″. *Courtesy of Betty Lou and Frank Gay.*

Paper sign for Old Virginia Cheroots, copyright 1899 by the American Tobacco Co. Signed F.N.Blue. 25″ x 17″. *Courtesy of Betty Lou and Frank Gay.*

An 1892 copyrighted sign for Old Virginia Cheroots. Signed F.N. Blue. 25" x 17". *Courtesy of Betty Lou and Frank Gay.*

Another hanging sign for American Tobacco's Old Virginia Cheroots. 10.5" x 6.25". *Courtesy of Betty Lou and Frank Gay.*

This pretty young woman encourages the smoking of Old Virginia Cheroots, "manufactured only by the Whitlock Branch of the America Tobacco Co., Richmond, Virginia." Taken from a copyrighted photo by E. Falk, New York. 10.5" x 6.50". *Courtesy of Betty Lou and Frank Gay.*

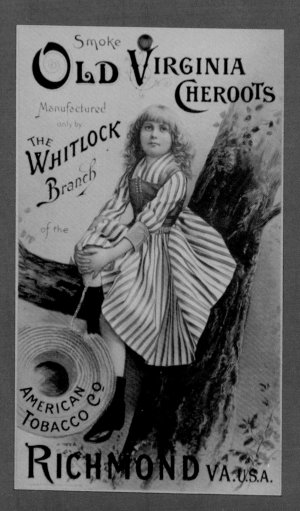

A poster from Piedmont Cigarettes, dated November 1, 1918, featuring the "first pictures of our boys at St. Mihiel." 12.75" x 19". *Courtesy of John & Elsie Booker, Patterson's Mill Country Store, Chapel Hill.*

A nicely done cardboard sign for J.B. Pace Tobacco Company's Vesta Cut Plug. 12.75" x 7.75". *Courtesy of Betty Lou and Frank Gay.*

Chas. W. Shonk Co., Chicago manufactured this self-framing tin sign for Paul Jones Havana Cigar. The cigars were manufactured by A.S. Valentine & Co., Philadelphia. 24" x 20". *Courtesy of Koehler Bros. Inc.—The General Store, Lafayette, Indiana.*

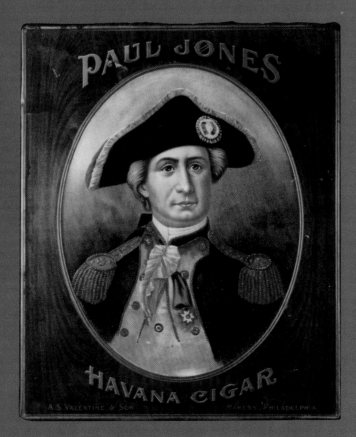

Tin string holder with cutter on the lid and advertising Red Bell Tobacco. 7" x 4" x 4". *Courtesy of Koehler Bros. Inc.--The General Store, Lafayette, Indiana.*

Saboroso cigar cutter and lighter. Cast iron and glass. *Courtesy of Betty Lou and Frank Gay.*

Wooden two-sided sidewalk sign for Scott Keltie cigars. 43" x 19" *Courtesy of Koehler Bros. Inc. — The General Store, Lafayette, Indiana.*

Left: 7" Seal of North Carolina lithographed tin, Marburg Bros., American Tobacco Company. Center: Greenback Smoking Tobacco pouch, 4", Marburg Bros. Right: cardboard Seal of North Carolina box, 2" x 7". *Courtesy of Betty Lou and Frank Gay.*

Humorous "Great Scott" poster for Seal of North Carolina Plug Cut, 8.5" x 6". Lithography by A. Hoen & Co., Baltimore. *Courtesy of Betty Lou and Frank Gay.*

"Great Scott No. 2" advertising Marburg's Greenback smoking tobacco. Cardboard, 7.75" x 12". *Courtesy of Betty Lou and Frank Gay.*

A series of beautifully illustrated posters for Seal of North Carolina tobacco. All have a European look and may have been designed to appeal to the growing immigrant population in the late 1800s and early 1900s. "Chrome-Heliograph" by A. Hoen & Co., Baltimore. 12.5" x 8". *Courtesy of Betty Lou and Frank Gay.*

Cigar and cigarette holder from the WDC company. Tin: 2″ x 9″. *Courtesy of Betty Lou and Frank Gay.*

Die cut paper figures mounted on wood stand guard for Sweet Caporal's Standard Cigarettes. 15″ x 5″. *Courtesy of Betty Lou and Frank Gay.*

Tobacco baskets hang on the wall on the Todd Country Store porch. *Courtesy of the Todd General Store, Todd, North Carolina.*

Die cut tin sign for U.S. Marine pipe tobacco. 6.5″ x 16″. *Courtesy of Betty Lou and Frank Gay.*

Tobacco cutter for Venable Chewing Tobacco, by Enterprise Manufacturing Co., Philadelphia. Patented April 15, 1875. &' x 16.5". *Courtesy of Betty Lou and Frank Gay.*

Tobacco cutter advertising the John Finzer & Brothers company, Louisville, Kentucky. Cast iron, 7" x 17". *Courtesy of Betty Lou and Frank Gay.*

A battle ax tobacco cutter of cast iron and wood. This nicely designed piece is 7.5" x 18". *Courtesy of Betty Lou and Frank Gay.*

This Dexter tobacco cutter measured the plug of tobacco and cut it. Wood and metal. *Courtesy of Koehler Bros. Inc.—The General Store, Lafayette, Indiana.*

SPIRITS

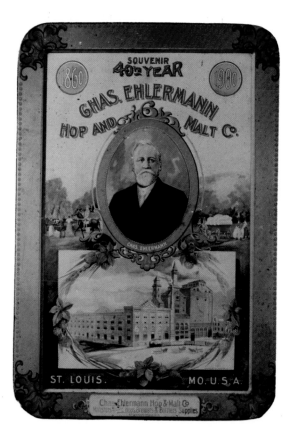

Truth in advertising may have begun with this 1899 small paper card for Green River whiskey. It "blots out all your troubles!" 4" x 9.5". *Courtesy of Koehler Bros. Inc.—The General Store, Lafayette, Indiana.*

Self-framing tin sign for Ehlermann Hop and Malt Co., St. Louis, Missouri. The sign was manufactured by Standard Advertising Company, Coshocton, Ohio, c. 1895. *Courtesy of Koehler Bros. Inc.—The General Store, Lafayette, Indiana.*

Much of the spirits that country stores carried were of the home-grown variety. This crock is from A.H. Harris Distiller, Atlanta, Georgia and measures 12" tall. *Courtesy of the Mast General Store, Valle Crucis, North Carolina.*

Fine reverse painted on glass sign for Rupert's Extra Beer. 27" x 25". *Courtesy of Betty Lou and Frank Gay.*

A crockery jug for Himmler & Co., Dealers in Pure Rye Whiskey, Cumberland, Maryland. 10″ tall. *Courtesy of Koehler Bros. Inc.—The General Store, Lafayette, Indiana.*

Self-framing tin sign for Monongahela Whiskey, made by Hamburger Distillery, Brownsville, Texas. *Courtesy of Koehler Bros. Inc.—The General Store, Lafayette, Indiana.*

Nice paper poster for Logan & Leach, proprietors of the Manhattan Cafe in Parkersburg, West Virginia. The whiskey on the table is Old Limestone. *Courtesy of Betty Lou and Frank Gay.*

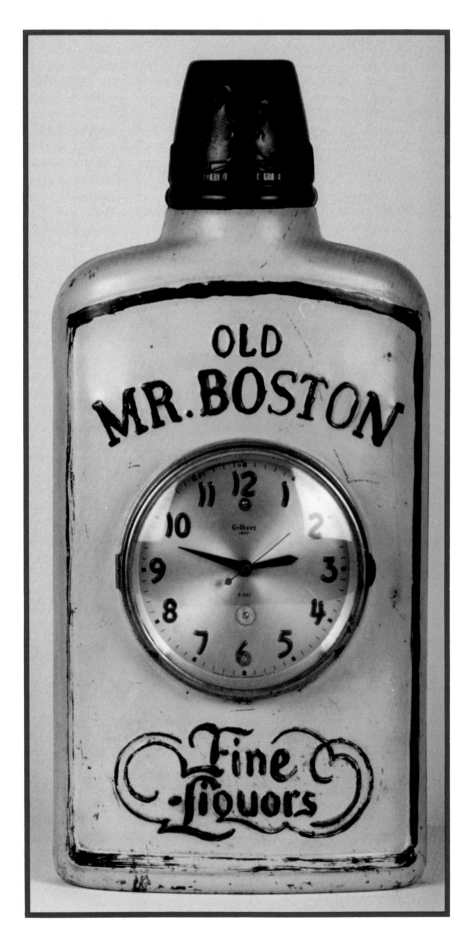

Old Mr. Boston advertising clock, metal, 22″ x 10″. The 8-day clock was made by Gilbert Clock, founded in 1807. *Courtesy of Koehler Bros. Inc.—The General Store, Lafayette, Indiana.*

Whiskey jug from Rose Distiller, Atlanta, Georgia. 13″ tall. *Courtesy of the Mast General Store, Valle Crucis, North Carolina.*

Chapter Five

Head to Toe, Inside and Out

CLOTHING

As factory-made clothes became more accepted, country stores were the chief source for these new outfits. While this suit is a bit fancy for a boy's everyday use, it would be a wonderful outfit for special occasions. The model is a wood frame set in cast iron boots to give it stability. 36″ tall. *Courtesy of Betty Lou and Frank Gay.*

A beautiful girl's dress on a composition pedestal model. 32.5″ tall. *Courtesy of Betty Lou and Frank Gay.*

Slant-front rack for Hank-O-Chief men's handkerchiefs. Wood and paper, 15" x 15.5" x 12". *Courtesy of Koehler Bros. Inc.--The General Store, Lafayette, Indiana.*

Oak and glass case for Brighton's 25-cent Garters. 19" x 12.5" x 10". *Courtesy of Koehler Bros. Inc.—The General Store, Lafayette, Indiana.*

Wood and paper display for Hickory Children's Garters, 20" x 13". *Courtesy of Hook's Historic Drug Store & Pharmacy Museum, Indianapolis.*

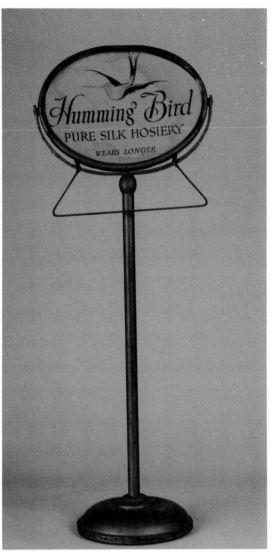

Stand for Humming Bird Stockings. Metal and paper, 20.5"
tall. *Courtesy of John & Elsie Booker, Patterson's Mill
Country Store, Chapel Hill.*

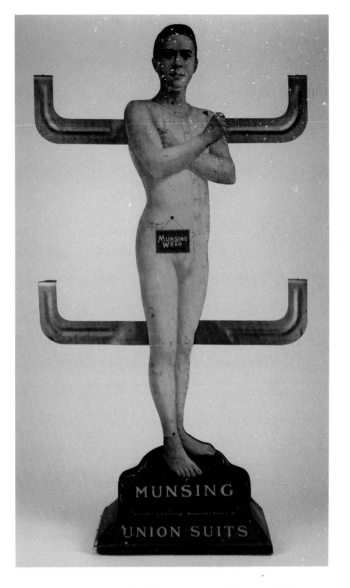

Tin Munsingwear display. 43.5" x
24". *Courtesy of Koehler Bros.
Inc.—The General Store,
Lafayette, Indiana.*

Papier mâche figure advertising
Lanb Knit, 15" x 16" x 6". *Courtesy
of Koehler Bros. Inc.—The
General Store, Lafayette, Indiana.*

Tin display for Munsing Union Suits. 45″ x 28″. *Courtesy of Koehler Bros. Inc.—The General Store, Lafayette, Indiana.*

The Ri-Co Muffler and box. *Courtesy of Betty Lou and Frank Gay.*

Wood and tin corner sign for Sweet-Orr & Co.'s Union-Made Overalls. 15″ x 10″. *Courtesy of Koehler Bros. Inc.—The General Store, Lafayette, Indiana.*

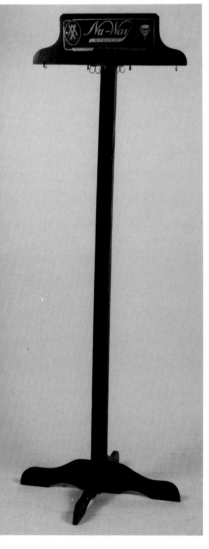

Wood display rack for Nu-Way Suspenders and Garters, 52″ x 17.5″. *Courtesy of Koehler Bros. Inc.—The General Store, Lafayette, Indiana.*

SHOES

Two piece lithographed tin Buster Brown display in excellent condition. Buster Brown, 39" tall, Tige, 23" tall. *Courtesy of Koehler Bros. Inc.—The General Store, Lafayette, Indiana.*

Buster Brown shoe display. Tin, 12" x 8". *Courtesy of Koehler Bros. Inc.—The General Store, Lafayette, Indiana.*

Tin Buster Brown Counter Display, American Art Works, Coshocton, Ohio. 24.5" x 22". *Courtesy of Koehler Bros. Inc.—The General Store, Lafayette, Indiana.*

An advertising fan for Buster Brown given away by J.P Kropp Shoe Store, Bladen, Nebraska. 14″ x 7.5″. *Courtesy of Koehler Bros. Inc.—The General Store, Lafayette, Indiana.*

Buster Brown stuffed cloth doll. 12.5″ x 6″. *Courtesy of Koehler Bros. Inc.— The General Store, Lafayette, Indiana.*

Buster Brown's White House shoes are advertised on this fan given away by the Chas. F. Spies shoe store, Boswell, Indiana. 13.5″ x 7.5″. *Courtesy of Koehler Bros. Inc.—The General Store, Lafayette, Indiana.*

A Buster Brown Camera with box. 4″ x 5.5″ x 5.5″. *Courtesy of Koehler Bros. Inc.—The General Store, Lafayette, Indiana.*

On this advertising fan, Buster Brown and Tige exchange a knowing wink as the ladies gather around to admire Buster's new shoes. Cardboard and wood, 14.5″ x 7.5″. *Courtesy of Koehler Bros. Inc.—The General Store, Lafayette, Indiana.*

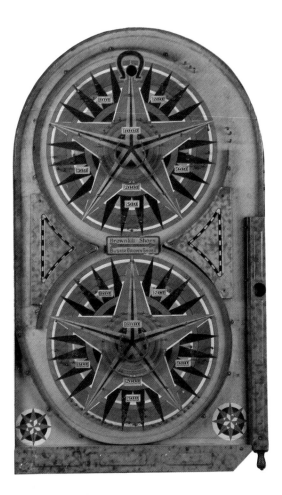

Tin stand for Peter's Diamond Brand Shoes, St. Louis, 16" x 10". *Courtesy of Betty Lou and Frank Gay.*

Tin and wood Buster Brown "Gold Star" game, manufactured by Lindstrom Tool & Toy Co., Bridgeport, Connecticut, c. 1934. This advertises Buster Brown Tread Straight Shoes. 24" x 14". *Courtesy of Koehler Bros. Inc.—The General Store, Lafayette, Indiana.*

Tin wall sign for W.L. Douglas Shoes. *Courtesy of Betty Lou and Frank Gay.*

Paper sign for Poll Parrot Shoes, 23.5" x 15.5". *Courtesy of Koehler Bros. Inc.—The General Store, Lafayette, Indiana.*

Poll Parrot Shoes sidewalk sign. 43.5" x 21.5". *Courtesy of Koehler Bros. Inc.—The General Store, Lafayette, Indiana.*

Tin and neon sign for Poll Parrot Shoes. *Courtesy of John & Elsie Booker, Patterson's Mill Country Store, Chapel Hill.*

Tin and wire string holder advertising Red Goose Shoes. *Courtesy of Betty Lou and Frank Gay.*

Embossed two-sided cardboard sign for Robin Hood Shoes. Free-standing, 15.5″ x 5″. *Courtesy of Koehler Bros. Inc.— The General Store, Lafayette, Indiana.*

Wire and wood shoe fitting stool, 14″ x 24″ x 10″. *Courtesy of John & Elsie Booker, Patterson's Mill Country Store, Chapel Hill.*

Pomeroy's Petroline Poroused Plasters tin, J. Ellwood Lee Co., Conshohocken, Pennsylvania. These plasters were used to apply medications which would be absorbed through the skin. 1″ x 8.5″ x 6″. *Courtesy of the Mast General Store, Valle Crucis, North Carolina.*

A die cut cardboard sign for Dr. Miles Nervine, featuring the image of a colonial woman. On the back she is identified as Dorothy (Dolly) Quincy, who married John Hancock in 1775. What she has to do with Dr. Miles Nervine is not made clear. 21″. *Courtesy of Betty Lou and Frank Gay.*

Walnut key wound clock with paper label for Reed's Tonic Cures. 25.25″. *Courtesy of Betty Lou and Frank Gay.*

Paper sign for Rexall Hair Tonic, 17.5″ x 22.5″. *Courtesy of Bob Biondi.*

Wonderful mirror sign for Syrup of Figs, California Fig Syrup Co., San Francisco, California. "Nature's own true laxative." *Courtesy of Betty Lou and Frank Gay.*

This wood and composition clock by Baird Clock Co., Plattsburgh, New York, advertises Vanner & Prest's "Molliscorium." Key wound, 29.75″. *Courtesy of Betty Lou and Frank Gay.*

Tin and glass display case for Armour's Fine Toilet Soaps, Chicago. 15″ x 16.5″ x 15″. *Courtesy of Koehler Bros. Inc.--The General Store, Lafayette, Indiana.*

Box for Fairbank's Pure, White, Floating, Fairy Soap. Wood with paper label, with litho by Q.H. Buek & Co., New York. 17″ x 16″ x 8″. *Courtesy of Koehler Bros. Inc.—The General Store, Lafayette, Indiana.*

Stand-up cardboard sign for Palmolive Shaving Cream, c. 1920s. Niagara Litho Co., Buffalo-Chicago, 34″ x 27″. *Courtesy of Koehler Bros. Inc.—The General Store, Lafayette, Indiana.*

Assorted facial and bath soaps. *Courtesy of John & Elsie Booker, Patterson's Mill Country Store, Chapel Hill.*

TOYS

Wood and paper doll's trunk, 10″ x 16″ x 9″. *Courtesy of Koehler Bros. Inc.—The General Store, Lafayette, Indiana.*

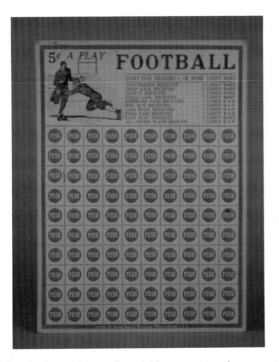

This football punchboard could have sat on the counter of the country store, waiting for some adventurous child to put down his 5 cents and take a chance on winning up to five candy bars. To avoid the tears of the losers, every child was guaranteed at least one candy bar. Cardboard, 10″ x 7.5″. *Courtesy of Betty Lou and Frank Gay.*

Dutch Wind Mill with box by the E.C. Peterson, Indianapolis. The vane is weight driven. 26″ x 10″. *Courtesy of Koehler Bros. Inc.—The General Store, Lafayette, Indiana.*

Puss in the Corner was one of Parker Brothers' first board games, being copyrighted in 1895. The object was to move all three of one's pieces from one side of the board to the other. The set included twelve wooden pieces and a metal spinner. Parker Brothers, Salem, Massachusetts, 7″ x 7″. *Courtesy of Hook's Historic Drug Store & Pharmacy Museum, Indianapolis.*

"The Funny Face Family" was a construction toy for children. This box contains Reddy, while other kits had Whitey, Bluey, and their pets. N. D. Cass Co., Athol, Massachusetts, 15″ x 7.5″. *Courtesy of Koehler Bros. Inc.— The General Store, Lafayette, Indiana.*

Tin grocery store. 14.5" x 30". *Courtesy of Koehler Bros. Inc. — The General Store, Lafayette, Indiana.*

Steel and wood Hubley pull truck, 6.5" x 23.5" x 7". *Courtesy of Koehler Bros. Inc. — The General Store, Lafayette, Indiana.*

Stenciled wooden doll cradle 9.5" x 18.75" x 9". *Courtesy of Koehler Bros. Inc. — The General Store, Lafayette, Indiana.*

Chapter Six

Everything for the Home, Road, and Farm

AROUND THE KITCHEN

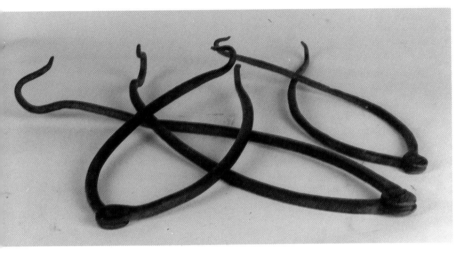

Cast iron pot hangers used to hold pots to hooks for fireplace cooking. 14"—19". *Courtesy of John & Elsie Booker, Patterson's Mill Country Store, Chapel Hill.*

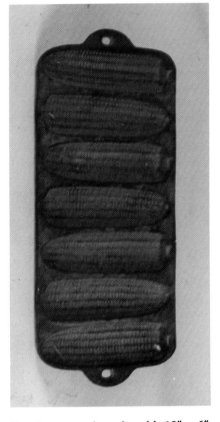

Cast iron corn bread mold, 12" x 6". *Courtesy of John & Elsie Booker, Patterson's Mill Country Store, Chapel Hill.*

Footed cast iron Dutch over. 2 ½ quarts, 7" x 18" x 10". *Courtesy of John & Elsie Booker, Patterson's Mill Country Store, Chapel Hill.*

Various cast iron cooking utensils. The frying pan is 9 inches in diameter with a 4" handle. The griddles are 20" x 9" and 22" x 10.5". *Courtesy of John & Elsie Booker, Patterson's Mill Country Store, Chapel Hill.*

Copper water heater with spigot. 15" tall x 13.5" in diameter. *Courtesy of the Mast General Store, Valle Crucis, North Carolina.*

Tin kettle with copper bottom, 10" tall x 9" in diameter. *Courtesy of Koehler Bros. Inc.—The General Store, Lafayette, Indiana.*

Majestic Copper Tea Kettle, 8" x 9.75". *Courtesy of Koehler Bros. Inc.—The General Store, Lafayette, Indiana.*

A collection of tin ware (l-r): dish, 2.75" x 10.25" x 7"; cake pan, 3" x 9"; canteen, 6.5" x 4"; colander, 4" x 9.5". *Courtesy of Koehler Bros. Inc. — The General Store, Lafayette, Indiana.*

Left: Coffee pot, 11" x 8". Middle: Milk pail, 10" x 6.5". Right: Crooked spout coffee pot: 10" x 7". *Courtesy of John & Elsie Booker, Patterson's Mill Country Store, Chapel Hill.*

Left-right: Bowl, 11" diameter; scoop, 15" long; pail, 9" x 11"; chamber pot, 5" x 9"; slop pan, 10" x 10"; pitcher, 9.5" x 10"; soap dish, 3" x 6.5" x 5". *Courtesy of John & Elsie Booker, Patterson's Mill Country Store, Chapel Hill.*

125

Graniteware tea and coffee kettles of various colors and styles. Left to right: Blue green tea pot, 6″ x 8″; green coffee pot, 10″ x 6″; gray crooked spout coffee pot, 8″ x 5.5″; gray coffee pot with embossed tin top, 9.5″ x 7″. *Courtesy of John & Elsie Booker, Patterson's Mill Country Store, Chapel Hill.*

Left: cast iron graniteware kettle with a pivot lid by Wrought Iron Range, St. Louis, 7″ x 9.5″. Right: green graniteware chamber pot, 11″ x 10″. *Courtesy of John & Elsie Booker, Patterson's Mill Country Store, Chapel Hill.*

Unusual graniteware forms (l-r): double boiler, 8″ x 6″; large funnel, 9.5″ x 9″; gray bucket, 9.5″ x 9″. *Courtesy of John & Elsie Booker, Patterson's Mill Country Store, Chapel Hill.*

Blue graniteware churn, 44″ x 11″. *Courtesy of Koehler Bros. Inc.—The General Store, Lafayette, Indiana.*

Gray graniteware pieces (l-r): covered casserole, 6" x 10"; double boiler, c. 1930s, 8" x 6.25"; colander, 3" x 9.75"; cake mold, 4.5" x 9". *Courtesy of Koehler Bros. Inc.—The General Store, Lafayette, Indiana.*

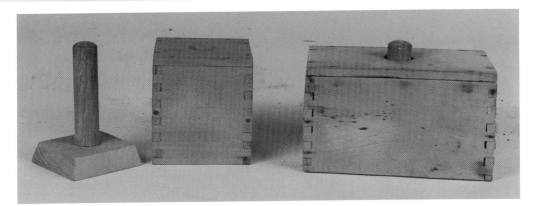

Wood butter molds, 3.25" tall. *Courtesy of John & Elsie Booker, Patterson's Mill Country Store, Chapel Hill.*

A No. 8 Universal Bread Maker by Landers, Frary, & Clark, New Britain, Connecticut. The crank turns a pastry hook inside. To use you place liquid with yeast and flour in the bucket and turn the crank for 3 minutes. After the dough rises, you turn the crank again until it forms a ball. Tin and cast iron. *Courtesy of John & Elsie Booker, Patterson's Mill Country Store, Chapel Hill.*

Primitive wood grinder with wood teeth on the wheel. This may have been used to make sausage. 12" x 14" x 8". *Courtesy of John & Elsie Booker, Patterson's Mill Country Store, Chapel Hill.*

127

Wood and screen sieves. 17", 11.5" and 10". *Courtesy of John & Elsie Booker, Patterson's Mill Country Store, Chapel Hill.*

Cracklin' press. To make cracklin', hog fat is cut in small squares and boiled down until as much grease as possible is removed. It is left to drain overnight, and then it is placed in the bucket and the lever is pushed. Lard is rendered through the holes, and what is left is cracklin'. This is browned and ground up to be used in bread. 39" x 42". *Courtesy of John & Elsie Booker, Patterson's Mill Country Store, Chapel Hill.*

Two slaw or kraut cutters. The left cutter is 19" x 7". The Indiana Kraut Cutter on the right was made by Tucker & Dorsey Mfg. Co., Indianapolis, 27" x 9". *Courtesy of Koehler Bros. Inc. — The General Store, Lafayette, Indiana.*

Pantry boxes, 4.5" deep, 9-10" in diameter. *Courtesy of Koehler Bros. Inc. — The General Store, Lafayette, Indiana.*

Brown stoneware jugs, 8.5"-10". *Courtesy of John & Elsie Booker, Patterson's Mill Country Store, Chapel Hill.*

Oak sugar bucket, 11.5". *Courtesy of Koehler Bros. Inc.—The General Store, Lafayette, Indiana.*

Stoneware jugs, 16", 10", 12.5". *Courtesy of John & Elsie Booker, Patterson's Mill Country Store, Chapel Hill.*

Special function crocks, 8"-9.5". Left: cookie jar. Middle: chicken feeder. Right: Syrup crock. *Courtesy of Koehler Bros. Inc.—The General Store, Lafayette, Indiana.*

Spongeware bowl, 7" x 14". Courtesy of Koehler Bros. Inc.—The General Store, Lafayette, Indiana.

Oak piggin bucket, 9" x 8". Courtesy of Koehler Bros. Inc.—The General Store, Lafayette, Indiana.

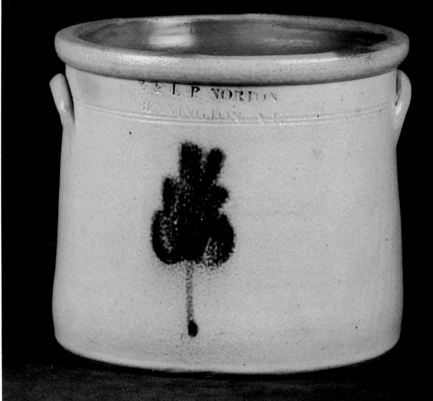

Bennington Norton Co. crock. 7" x 8.5". Courtesy of Koehler Bros. Inc.— The General Store, Lafayette, Indiana.

Pottery bowls, 6.75"-8.75" in diameter. Courtesy of Koehler Bros. Inc.—The General Store, Lafayette, Indiana.

Left: Six gallon crock with vine, 17″ x 11″. Right: Two gallon crock marked Hamilton, MA, Jones, Green, & Bond, 10″ x 9″. *Courtesy of Koehler Bros. Inc.—The General Store, Lafayette, Indiana.*

LAUNDRY DAY

Assorted laundry products (l-r): Oxydol, Proctor & Gamble, 6″; PDQ Blue (tin), 3.25″; Keen's Oxford Blue, 1.25″; Safford's DX-1, the Safford Co., Burnville, North Carolina, 5″; Peerless Washing Tablets, 2″; Diamond Blue (tin), John Diamond & Sons, 3″; Kuttyhunk Bluing, Diamond, McDonnell & Co., Philadelphia, 4.5″; Soapine, Kendall Mfg. Co., Providence, Rhode Island, 5.75″; Success Soda, Morehouse Mfg. Co., Savannah, Georgia (paper), 4.5″. *Courtesy of John & Elsie Booker, Patterson's Mill Country Store, Chapel Hill.*

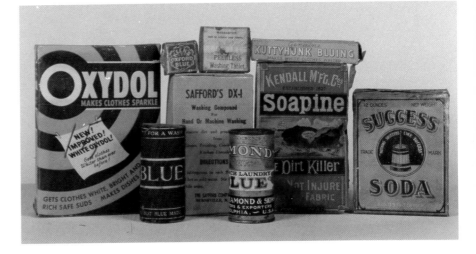

Advertising card for American Bluing Company, Buffalo, New York, 10.5". *Courtesy of Koehler Bros. Inc.—The General Store, Lafayette, Indiana.*

Left: later Gold Dust tin marked Lever Brothers Company, Cambridge, Massachusetts, 4.75". Right: 2.75" Gold Dust tin marked Fairbank's Gold Dust Corp., New York, St. Louis, and Montreal. *Courtesy of John & Elsie Booker, Patterson's Mill Country Store, Chapel Hill.*

Embossed tin for Silver Gloss Starch, Edwardsburg Starch Co., Cardinal, Ontario. The Thomas Davidson Mfg. Co., Montreal, Quebec, 8.25". *Courtesy of Betty Lou and Frank Gay.*

Gold Dust cardboard case, 12.5" x 18.5" x 11". *Courtesy of Koehler Bros. Inc.—The General Store, Lafayette, Indiana.*

The Boss Perfection No. 4 washer. Wood, 36" x 33" x 21". *Courtesy of John & Elsie Booker, Patterson's Mill Country Store, Chapel Hill.*

The oak Hand Lever Home Washer by the Miller Manufacturing Co., Meyersdale, Pennsylvania, 26" x 25". The wringer is by Boss.

Copper laundry pot, 15" x 27" x 13". *Courtesy of John & Elsie Booker, Patterson's Mill Country Store, Chapel Hill.*

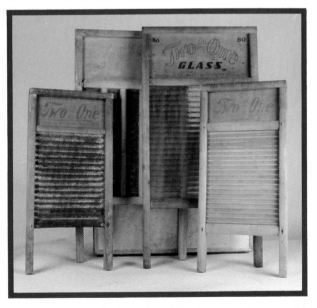

Two-in-One wash boards with glass or brass rubbing surfaces. Carolina Washboard Co., Raleigh. 18"-24". *Courtesy of John & Elsie Booker, Patterson's Mill Country Store, Chapel Hill.*

Hand wash agitators. The one on the left is all wood with five legs, 34". The washer twists the agitator side back-and-forth while pushing it up-and-down. The agitator on the right is 45" long and has a spring loaded tin agitator on the end to help move the clothes around in the tub. *Courtesy of John & Elsie Booker, Patterson's Mill Country Store, Chapel Hill.*

The Hartford Folding Bench held a mechanical wringer at the top. The clothes would be run through wringer from the laundry tub on one side to basket on the other, ready to be hung on the line. Lovett Mfg., Erie Pennsylvania. 39" x 76" when open. *Courtesy of John & Elsie Booker, Patterson's Mill Country Store, Chapel Hill.*

Assorted flat irons, 3.5"-6". *Courtesy of John & Elsie Booker, Patterson's Mill Country Store, Chapel Hill.*

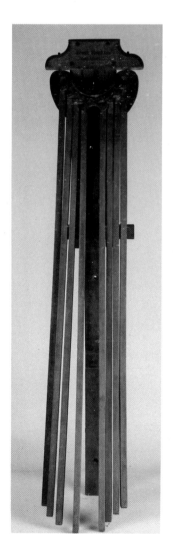

Folding clothes drying rack by Fred Hopkins. 36". *Courtesy of John & Elsie Booker, Patterson's Mill Country Store, Chapel Hill.*

After generations of heating an iron in the fire or on the stove, the 19th and early twentieth centuries saw some innovation. The iron on the left was heated by kerosene, the center iron would hold hot coals, and the iron on the right is an early electric iron made by the Chicago Flexible Shaft Co. *Courtesy of John & Elsie Booker, Patterson's Mill Country Store, Chapel Hill.*

Opposite page bottom left:
Liquid Veneer display box, 33.5" x 13.5" x 10.5". This tin box was made by the H.D. Beach Co., Coshocton, Ohio. *Courtesy of Koehler Bros. Inc.—The General Store, Lafayette, Indiana.*

HOUSEHOLD GOODS

Home Tacks display box from the Task Corporation, Boston. The lithography was by Lindner, Eddy & Claus Litho, New York. Made of cardboard, the large box measures 2″ x 9.5″ x 8″ and the smaller boxes are 1.75″ x 2.25″ x 2.5″. *Courtesy of John & Elsie Booker, Patterson's Mill Country Store, Chapel Hill.*

An assortment of fire extinguishers. Tin and paper, 22″. *Courtesy of Betty Lou and Frank Gay.*

This galvanized tub was featured in the Sears catalogue of 1908. It has cast iron supports and is trimmed in oak. 24″ x 54″ x 28″. *Courtesy of John & Elsie Booker, Patterson's Mill Country Store, Chapel Hill.*

Wood commode with chamber pot. 17" x 24" x 13". *Courtesy of John & Elsie Booker, Patterson's Mill Country Store, Chapel Hill.*

Left: a country broom with bristles of oak shavings. Right: a corn shuck mop. Corn shucks were forced into the holes, creating a good, strong cleaning surface. 60". *Courtesy of John & Elsie Booker, Patterson's Mill Country Store, Chapel Hill.*

Store rack for Merkle's Blu-Jay Brooms. Steel with embossed tin signs, 35" x 10" x 23". *Courtesy of Koehler Bros. Inc.—The General Store, Lafayette, Indiana.*

Bissell Sweeper and display rack. Made of oak with a paper sign the rack measures 46" x 17". *Courtesy of Koehler Bros. Inc.—The General Store, Lafayette, Indiana.*

Three Bon Ami products: a cleanser tin, 5″ and soap bars for household cleaning, 2.25″ and 3.75″. Bon Ami Company, New York. *Courtesy of John & Elsie Booker, Patterson's Mill Country Store, Chapel Hill.*

Assorted cleansers (l-r): Bab-O Cleanser, B.T. Babbitt, Inc., New York, 4.75″; Annette's Perfect Cleanser Co., Boston; Old Dutch Cleanser, Cudahy Soap Works, Chicago, 5″; Octagon Cleanser, Palmolive Peat Co., New Jersey, 4.5″. *Courtesy of John & Elsie Booker, Patterson's Mill Country Store, Chapel Hill.*

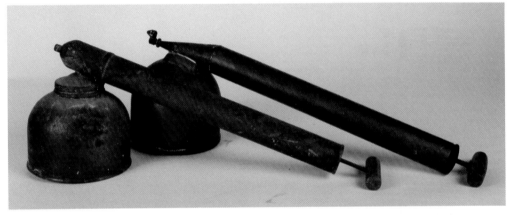

These copper and brass sprayers should have helped get rid of household pest. 6″ x 19″ x 5″. *Courtesy of John & Elsie Booker, Patterson's Mill Country Store, Chapel Hill.*

Bar soaps. Top: Sunset Soap Dye, North American Dye Corporation, Mt. Vernon, New York, 2.75″ x 1″. Left: P & G, Proctor & Gamble. Right: Colgate's Octagon Soap, Colgate-Palmolive Co., New York, 4.25″ x 1″. *Courtesy of John & Elsie Booker, Patterson's Mill Country Store, Chapel Hill.*

A four hole mouse trap. When loaded the wire noose is down. When the mouse goes for the bait, the noose comes up choking him. Gory but effective. This early model is of wood and wire. *Courtesy of Betty Lou and Frank Gay.*

137

Where did country musicians get their strings? They either made them or went to the country store. This is a tin case for W & S Keystone State Strings. Tin and glass, 24" x 16.5" x 14". *Courtesy of Koehler Bros. Inc.—The General Store, Lafayette, Indiana.*

When the phonograph made it to the country, the country store was there to market it. This is an Edison Standard, serial number 620470. Made in Orange, New Jersey, the base measures 12" x 12" x 8.5". The megaphone is 36" long. *Courtesy of John & Elsie Booker, Patterson's Mill Country Store, Chapel Hill.*

Glass and metal display case for Stafford Superfine Ink, 26" x 25" x 14". *Courtesy of Koehler Bros. Inc.—The General Store, Lafayette, Indiana.*

An Edison Gold Molded Record, 1904. Paper packaging with a hard rubber cylinder. 4.5" x 2.75". *Courtesy of Koehler Bros. Inc.—The General Store, Lafayette, Indiana.*

Assorted writing and typing supplies *Courtesy of John & Elsie Booker, Patterson's Mill Country Store, Chapel Hill.*

Tin dispensing case for Eversharp Leads. Specialty Display Case Co., Kendallville, Indiana, 8.5" x 14.25" x 4.25". *Courtesy of John & Elsie Booker, Patterson's Mill Country Store, Chapel Hill.*

Sanford's Inks display rack. Oak and glass, 16" x 12.5" x 11". *Courtesy of Koehler Bros. Inc.—The General Store, Lafayette, Indiana.*

139

DYES AND NOTIONS

Angel Dainty Dyes display case. Tin with a wood base, 18" x 14" x 6". *Courtesy of Koehler Bros. Inc.—The General Store, Lafayette, Indiana.*

The prismatic diamond in the center of this illustration is an apt symbol for Diamond Dyes. The oak cabinet was built by Kellogg & Burkeley Co. and is 30" x 22.5" x 10". *Courtesy of Koehler Bros. Inc.—The General Store, Lafayette, Indiana.*

This Diamond Dyes display case features and embossed tin front in nice condition. 24" x 15.5" x 7.5". *Courtesy of Koehler Bros. Inc.—The General Store, Lafayette, Indiana.*

The same illustration was used on a Diamond Dye display of a later, different design. Oak, 14" x 12.5" x 8". *Courtesy of Koehler Bros. Inc.—The General Store, Lafayette, Indiana.*

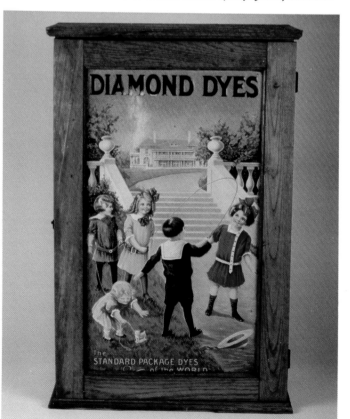

This nice wooden case is for Rainbow Dyes and features a rainbow in the arch at the top. Wood with transfer graphics. 19" x 11" x 7". *Courtesy of Koehler Bros. Inc.—The General Store, Lafayette, Indiana.*

Tin and wood Rit Dye Case, c. 1920. 16.25" x 14" x 11". *Courtesy of Koehler Bros. Inc.—The General Store, Lafayette, Indiana.*

A nice case for Turkish Dyes. Wood, 28" x 17" x 10". *Courtesy of Koehler Bros. Inc.—The General Store, Lafayette, Indiana.*

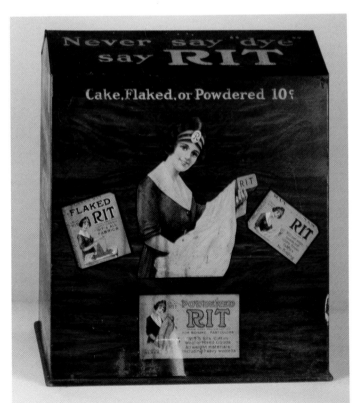

Wood and glass case for Clark's O.N.T. Embroidery floss. 13" x 18.5" x 19.25". *Courtesy of John & Elsie Booker, Patterson's Mill Country Store, Chapel Hill.*

A wonderful oak case for J & P Coats Spool Cotton. 23" x 21.5" x 16". *Courtesy of John & Elsie Booker, Patterson's Mill Country Store, Chapel Hill.*

This nice J & P Coats spool cabinet has four embossed wooden drawers and handsome original brasses. It measures 19" x 17" x 22". *Courtesy of Koehler Bros. Inc.—The General Store, Lafayette, Indiana.*

J & P Coats used several varieties of this clever counter case in the shape of a spool of thread. This is a small, single draw unit of wood and fabric, which measures 10" x 10" x 15.5". *Courtesy of Koehler Bros. Inc.—The General Store, Lafayette, Indiana.*

Self-standing cardboard sign for Coats & Clark's threads. 16" x 9.5". *Courtesy of John & Elsie Booker, Patterson's Mill Country Store, Chapel Hill.*

A cast iron, hand-operated sewing machine. 10″ x 12″ x 8″. *Courtesy of John & Elsie Booker, Patterson's Mill Country Store, Chapel Hill.*

The other necessity for the home seamstress was good cutlery. Country stores carried a variety of scissors to meet that need. This walnut and glass case is marked "Nickel Plated Scissors & Shears, Every Pair Warranted." 28″ x 14″ x 14″. *Courtesy of Koehler Bros. Inc.—The General Store, Lafayette, Indiana.*

This spinning wheel was manufactured in Falling Rock, Pennsylvania. 37″ x 18″. *Courtesy of John & Elsie Booker, Patterson's Mill Country Store, Chapel Hill.*

Early electric Singer Sewing machine with its bent-wood case. Catalog number B.U.7A. 12″ x 17″ x 8.25″. *Courtesy of John & Elsie Booker, Patterson's Mill Country Store, Chapel Hill.*

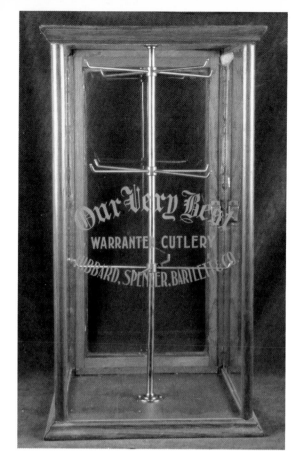

This case for Griffon Cutlery was manufactured by H. Pauk & Sons, St. Louis. 17.5" x 38" x 26". *Courtesy of Koehler Bros. Inc.—The General Store, Lafayette, Indiana.*

A nice case for Hubbard, Spencer, Bartlett & Co. cutlery, "Our Very Best." Oak with etched glass and a brass display rack. 26" x 14" x 14". *Courtesy of Koehler Bros. Inc.—The General Store, Lafayette, Indiana.*

HARDWARE

This revolving bolt cabinet has forty drawers. Octagonal wood construction, 39" x 23" x 23". *Courtesy of John & Elsie Booker, Patterson's Mill Country Store, Chapel Hill.*

Wood nail bins still in use at the Mast store. 45" x 65". *Courtesy of the Mast General Store, Valle Crucis, North Carolina.*

144

The octagonal top of this bolt cabinet sits atop a base with drawers. Wood, 58" tall. *Courtesy of the Mast General Store, Valle Crucis, North Carolina.*

Wood rope winder. *Courtesy of John & Elsie Booker, Patterson's Mill Country Store, Chapel Hill.*

This wonderful near life-size tin display for Van Camp Hardware and Iron Co., Indianapolis, is three dimensional, c. 1920-1930. The bench is about 12" deep and holds real tools. The whole piece is 60" tall and 42" wide. Shonk Works, Maywood, Illinois. *Courtesy of Koehler Bros. Inc.— The General Store, Lafayette, Indiana.*

The Kent Kinfa Sharpener has a wheel inside lined with sharpening stones and leather for honing. The knife is inserted in the appropriate hole and the wheel is turned to give it a nice edge. London, 18" x 17" x 5". *Courtesy of John & Elsie Booker, Patterson's Mill Country Store, Chapel Hill.*

This ball bearing advertisement is cardboard and stands 60″ tall. *Courtesy of Koehler Bros. Inc.— The General Store, Lafayette, Indiana.*

Block and tackle were everyday equipment for the farms and businesses that patronized the country store. *Courtesy of John & Elsie Booker, Patterson's Mill Country Store, Chapel Hill.*

Life-sized cardboard sign for Pritchard-Strong Co. The lithography is by the Stecher Co., Rochester, New York. 60″ x 37.5″. *Courtesy of Koehler Bros. Inc.—The General Store, Lafayette, Indiana.*

A wide assortment of tools could be found at the store. The inventory was developed around the local needs, and was usually limited to the most basic tools. *Courtesy of John & Elsie Booker, Patterson's Mill Country Store, Chapel Hill.*

Folding stand-up sign for Nicholson Files, Nicholson File Co., Providence, Rhode Island. The Munro & Harford Co., New York. Cardboard, 39" x 55". *Courtesy of Koehler Bros. Inc.—The General Store, Lafayette, Indiana.*

LIGHTING

Eveready Flashlights and Batteries poster. Frederick Sta(u)ley, artist. *Courtesy of John & Elsie Booker, Patterson's Mill Country Store, Chapel Hill.*

147

Tin candle mold, 10.75″ tall. *Courtesy of the Mast General Store, Valle Crucis, North Carolina.*

Left: Regal lantern, 13.5″ x 6″. Right: Paull's Leader/Gold Blast, 15″ x 7″. *Courtesy of John & Elsie Booker, Patterson's Mill Country Store, Chapel Hill.*

Adlake Non-Sweating Lamp, Chicago, 16″ x 7″. *Courtesy of John & Elsie Booker, Patterson's Mill Country Store, Chapel Hill.*

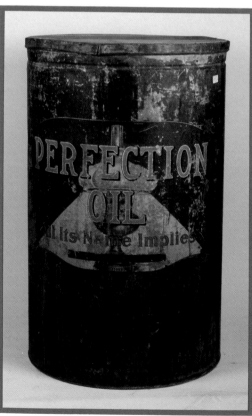

A common fixture in the country store was the lamp oil barrel. This Perfection Oil barrel is steel, measuring 36.5″ tall x 23.5″ in diameter. *Courtesy of Koehler Bros. Inc.— The General Store, Lafayette, Indiana.*

Tin and glass Kwik-Lite Flashlight Display. 6.5" x 16" x 14". *Courtesy of Koehler Bros. Inc.—The General Store, Lafayette, Indiana.*

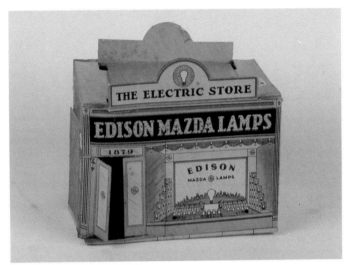

Tin and glass oil lamp, 16". *Courtesy of Koehler Bros. Inc.—The General Store, Lafayette, Indiana.*

Cardboard store display for Mazda lamps. 9" x 8" x 6". *Courtesy of Koehler Bros. Inc.—The General Store, Lafayette, Indiana.*

Miller Regalite coach lantern. Tin, 6" x 7" x 4". *Courtesy of John & Elsie Booker, Patterson's Mill Country Store, Chapel Hill.*

Dietz Union Driving Lamp, New York. Tin, 12" x 6". *Courtesy of John & Elsie Booker, Patterson's Mill Country Store, Chapel Hill.*

149

AUTOMOBILES

Self-framing tin sign for the Portage Rubber Co., Akron, Ohio. 25.5″ x 38″. R.J. Kennedy, artist. *Courtesy of Koehler Bros. Inc.—The General Store, Lafayette, Indiana.*

This galvanized water container pivots in its frame for ease of pouring. 14″ x 14″ x 11″. *Courtesy of John & Elsie Booker, Patterson's Mill Country Store, Chapel Hill.*

Swingspout Measure copper oil can with cockvalve in the spout for control. Swingspout Measure Co., 10.5″ x 8″ x 4.5″. *Courtesy of John & Elsie Booker, Patterson's Mill Country Store, Chapel Hill.*

1, 2, and 4 quart Dover Oil cans. The 1 quart can has lines for mixing gas and oil. Tin, 8″, 10″, and 12″. *Courtesy of John & Elsie Booker, Patterson's Mill Country Store, Chapel Hill.*

Rack of eight oil bottles made by the Master Mfg. Co., Litchfield, Illinois. 18″ x 14″ x 9″. *Courtesy of John & Elsie Booker, Patterson's Mill Country Store, Chapel Hill.*

FARM NEEDS

Three tin pitchers, 5″-8″. *Courtesy of John & Elsie Booker, Patterson's Mill Country Store, Chapel Hill.*

"Magic" gas and/or oil cans. Tin, 10″ -12″.

Cast iron Lansdowne Milking Stool, Cherry Bassett Co., 10″ x 9.5″. *Courtesy of John & Elsie Booker, Patterson's Mill Country Store, Chapel Hill.*

An unusual covered milk pail. Tin, 12″ x 11″. *Courtesy of John & Elsie Booker, Patterson's Mill Country Store, Chapel Hill.*

Milk can from Durham Dairy Products, Durham, North Carolina. 21″ x 11″. *Courtesy of John & Elsie Booker, Patterson's Mill Country Store, Chapel Hill.*

Oak and steel White's Cylinder Churn, c. 1900. 15.5″ x 13″. *Courtesy of John & Elsie Booker, Patterson's Mill Country Store, Chapel Hill.*

Small milk pail, 9.5″ x 6.5″. *Courtesy of John & Elsie Booker, Patterson's Mill Country Store, Chapel Hill.*

A wooden three-gallon axle-crank churn by George H. Spain, c. 1900. 16″ x 16″ x 12″. *Courtesy of John & Elsie Booker, Patterson's Mill Country Store, Chapel Hill.*

Pine stave churns with wood or iron bands were among the earliest used in America. This Dasher churn dates to about 1900. The base is 18″ tall, while the overall height is 30″. *Courtesy of John & Elsie Booker, Patterson's Mill Country Store, Chapel Hill.*

A McCormick Deering separator, made by International Harvester Co., Chicago. 49″. *Courtesy of John & Elsie Booker, Patterson's Mill Country Store, Chapel Hill.*

This stoneware Dasher churns were the most popular home models. These models hold 2-3 gallons. The bases measure 16" tall, with an overall height of 34". *Courtesy of John & Elsie Booker, Patterson's Mill Country Store, Chapel Hill.*

Wooden churn, 31" x 16". *Courtesy of Koehler Bros. Inc.-- The General Store, Lafayette, Indiana.*

One attempt at making churning an easier chore was this Superior Sanitary Churn, c. 1910. The mechanism set the churn spinning end-over-end while the churner gave small pushes on the handle. Superior Churn & Mfg. Co., Northville, Michigan. *Courtesy of John & Elsie Booker, Patterson's Mill Country Store, Chapel Hill.*

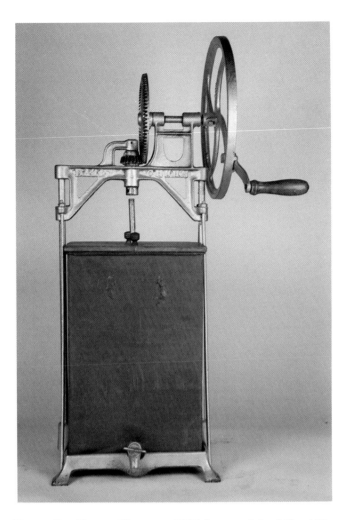

W.C. Hudson of Chapel Hill devised this belt-driven churn for his farm, c. 1920. 57″ tall. *Courtesy of John & Elsie Booker, Patterson's Mill Country Store, Chapel Hill.*

Five-gallon Dazey Churn, c. 1907. Iron and tin, 31″ x 10″ x 10″. *Courtesy of John & Elsie Booker, Patterson's Mill Country Store, Chapel Hill.*

This suspended churn did its work by swinging back and forth. Wood with stencilling, Bellows Falls, Pennsylvania. *Courtesy of John & Elsie Booker, Patterson's Mill Country Store, Chapel Hill.*

One gallon cranking Dazey Churn, c. 1922. It was used in the kitchen to churn milk from the farm or from vendors. Dazey Churn Co., St. Louis, 14″ x 6″ x 6″. *Courtesy of John & Elsie Booker, Patterson's Mill Country Store, Chapel Hill.*

A later model Dazey Churn jar shows the streamlining influence in both the crank and the jar. Dazey Churn Co., St. Louis, 16″ x 10″. *Courtesy of John & Elsie Booker, Patterson's Mill Country Store, Chapel Hill.*

A tin chicken feeder and water bottle. *Courtesy of John & Elsie Booker, Patterson's Mill Country Store, Chapel Hill.*

The leather horse collar was a necessity for the farmer and the country store was sure to have a supply of various sizes on hand. *Courtesy of John & Elsie Booker, Patterson's Mill Country Store, Chapel Hill.*

With electricity came electric appliances like this churn. The Dixie Maid mechanism is by Southern Electric Products, Anderson, S. Carolina. The Gem Dandy Jar is by Alabama Manufacturing, Birmingham, Alabama. *Courtesy of John & Elsie Booker, Patterson's Mill Country Store, Chapel Hill.*

Mechanical corn shucker. The husked ear of corn was placed in the chute at the top, and with a few turn of the handle the kernels were removed and deposited in a waiting pail. Wood and iron. *Courtesy of John & Elsie Booker, Patterson's Mill Country Store, Chapel Hill.*

Tin self-standing sign for Dr. LeGear veterinary medicines, Dr. L.D. LeGear Medicine Company. 14.5" x 17.75". *Courtesy of Koehler Bros. Inc.—The General Store, Lafayette, Indiana.*

For wagons going over the rough terrain of farm or country road, a wagon jack was a necessity. Wood and iron, 30" x 22". *Courtesy of John & Elsie Booker, Patterson's Mill Country Store, Chapel Hill.*

Cotton card for cleaning cotton and stretching it into strands for spinning. Watson-Williams Mfg. Co., Leicester, Massachusetts. *Courtesy of John & Elsie Booker, Patterson's Mill Country Store, Chapel Hill.*

Oval self-framing tin sign for Squire's Feed, John P. Squire & Company, Boston, 1906. 23″ x 20″. *Courtesy of Koehler Bros. Inc.—The General Store, Lafayette, Indiana.*

Oak and glass cabinet for Corona Wool Fat for Horses and Cows. 23.5″ x 14″ x 9″. *Courtesy of Koehler Bros. Inc.— The General Store, Lafayette, Indiana.*

Miniature chest-shaped counter advertising piece for Wilbur's Vegetable Horse, Cattle, Hog & Poultry Food. Wood, 10″ x 5″ x 5″. *Courtesy of Koehler Bros. Inc.—The General Store, Lafayette, Indiana.*

Tin cabinet for Sergeant's Dog Medicines, 14″ x 12″. *Courtesy of Betty Lou and Frank Gay.*

Blackman's Medicated Salt Brick stand, Blackman Stock Medicine Co., Chattanooga, Tennessee. Wood, 31". *Courtesy of Betty Lou and Frank Gay.*

One clever gadget you may have found at the country store was the Owen's Automatic transplanter. This tin machine would scoop up a seedling, and transplant it with a little dose of fertilizer at the pull of a trigger. B. Owen Co., Brookneal, Virginia, 28" x 12". *Courtesy of John & Elsie Booker, Patterson's Mill Country Store, Chapel Hill.*

Philips' Seeds box, Philips' Seeds, Mercerville, Pennsylvania, 5" x 25" x 11". Wood and paper, 5" x 25" x 11". *Courtesy of John & Elsie Booker, Patterson's Mill Country Store, Chapel Hill.*

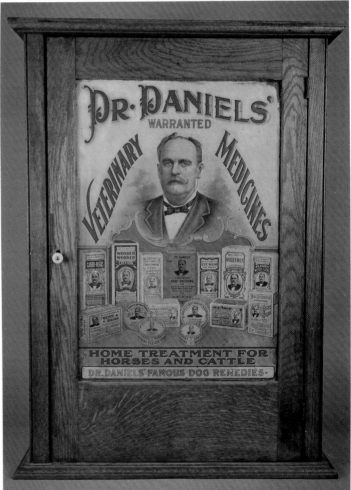

Oak and tin sign for Dr. Daniel's Veterinary Medicines. *Courtesy of Betty Lou and Frank Gay.*

Bibliography

Clark, Thomas D. *Pills, Petticoats, & Plows: The Southern Country Store*. Norman, Oklahoma: University of Oklahoma Press, 1944 (third printing 1989).

Congdon-Martin, Douglas, with Bob Biondi. *Country Store Collectibles*. West Chester: Schiffer Publishing Ltd., 1990.

Congdon-Martin, Douglas. *America For Sale: A Collector's Guide to Antique Advertising*. West Chester: Schiffer Publishing Ltd., 1991.

————. *Drugstore and Soda Fountain Antiques* West Chester: Schiffer Publishing Ltd., 1991.

Grossholz, Roselyn. *Country Store Collectibles* Des Moines, Iowa: Wallace-Homestead Book Company, 1972.

Heise, Ulla. *Coffee and Coffee Houses*. West Chester, Pa.: Schiffer Publishing, Ltd., 1987.

Hornsby, Peter R.G. *Decorated Biscuit Tins*. West Chester, Pa.: Schiffer Publishing, Ltd., 1984.

Johnson, Laurence A. *Over the Counter and On the Shelf, Country Storekeeping in America, 1620-1920*. Rutland, Vt.: Charles E. Tuttle Company: Publishers, 1961.

Ketchum, William Jr. *The Catalog of America Collectibles*. New York: Mayflower Books Inc. and Rutledge Books, Inc., 1979.

Kilpatrick, Frank. *How to Run a Country Store*. Pownal, Vt.: Storey Communications, Inc., 1986.

Klug, Ray. *Encyclopedia of Antique Advertising, Volume II*. West Chester, Pa.: Schiffer Publishing, Ltd., 1985.

McClinton, Katharine M. *The Complete Book of American Country Antiques*. New York: Conrad-McCann, Inc., 1967.

Raycraft, Donald R. *Early American Folk and Country Antiques*, Rutland, Vt: Charles E. Tuttle Company, Publishers, 1971.

Raycraft, Don and Carol. *Price Guide to American Country Antiques, 5th Edition*. Lombard, Ill.: Wallace-Homestead Book Company, 1985.

Raycraft, Don and Carol. *Price Guide to American Country Antiques, 8th Edition*. Radnor, Pa.: Wallace-Homestead Book Company, 1988.

Raycraft, Don and Carol. *The Collector's Guide to Kitchen Antiques*. Paducah, Ky.: Collector Books, 1981.

Wood, James Playsted. *The Story of Advertising*. New York: The Ronald Press Company, 1958.